JOHNNY DEPP

JOHNNY DEPP
The Illustrated Biography

Nick Johnstone

CARLTON
BOOKS

THIS IS
A CARLTON BOOK

This edition published in
2008 by Carlton Books Ltd
20 Mortimer Street
London W1T 3JW

First published by Carlton
Books Ltd in 2006

Text and design copyright
© Carlton Books Ltd 2008

ISBN 978-1-84732-160-2

Editorial Manager: Lorna Russell
Project Editor: Lara Maiklem/
Cressida Malins
Art Director: Lucy Coley/Mark
Cavanagh
Design: Barbara Zuñiga
Production: Lisa French/
Janette Burgin

Printed in Dubai

B
D4233jo

Contents

Introduction

'Great actor', 'bad boy', 'cool', 'rebel', 'troubled heart throb', 'Hollywood outsider', 'teen idol', 'chameleon', 'contented dad', 'maverick'

These are just some of the tags synonymous with Johnny Depp. Across a twenty-year career, he's become one of the finest actors of his generation, mostly playing an incredible, eclectic array of tongue-tied misfits, sensitive outsiders and eccentric renegades. Starting with his breakthrough performance in *Edward Scissorhands* (1990) and climaxing in 2003 with his role as Captain Jack Sparrow in *Pirates of the Caribbean: The Curse of the Black Pearl*, Depp's offbeat choice of parts has confounded and delighted critics and fans alike. Along the way this strong-minded actor, who has consistently prioritized artistic integrity over commercial appeal, famously turned down a slew of parts in massive box-office smashes like *Speed* (1994), *Titanic* (1997), *Interview with the Vampire* (1994) and *Indecent Proposal* (1993). Instead he chose small, acclaimed independent films he believed in, such as *Arizona Dream* (1993), *Dead Man* (1995) and *Benny & Joon* (1993).

Depp's fascination with offbeat roles was partly motivated by the experience of being turned into a teen idol and pin-up when he starred in the TV show *21 Jump Street* (1987–91). On leaving the show in 1990 (a move emboldened by his meeting with director and kindred spirit Tim Burton that led to him landing the lead role in *Edward Scissorhands*), he was determined thereon to only take parts to which he could relate, such as *What's Eating Gilbert Grape* (1993), *Ed Wood* (1994) and *Fear and Loathing in Las Vegas* (1998).

Even if his film roles to date have been determinedly anti-commercial, Depp's personal life has long been the subject of mainstream media fascination. During his stint on *21 Jump Street*, in interviews he spoke candidly of a wild adolescence spent playing in bands, experimenting with drugs and dropping out of high school, building a myth for himself that led reporters to talk him up as a new James Dean. Then, after marrying and divorcing at a young age and dating actresses Sherilyn Fenn and Jennifer Grey, Depp's relationship with actress Winona Ryder, which ran parallel to his ever-rising celebrity, was played out to a tireless gallery of paparazzi and tabloid reporters.

Under constant pressure from the unwelcome attention and widespread unwanted fame, Depp sought comfort in periods of heavy drinking. His next relationship, with supermodel Kate Moss, was also played out under a media microscope and in 1994 over-zealous scrutiny led him to famously trash a suite at New York's exclusive Mark Hotel. Intimate friendships with legendary hellraisers like Hunter S. Thompson, Keith Richards, Shane MacGowan, Iggy Pop and Marlon Brando sealed his reputation as a Hollywood rebel.

But all that has changed and 2008 finds Johnny Depp personally content and at the top of his profession. Riding high with *Pirates of the Caribbean: At World's End* (the third installment of the enormously successful *Pirates of the Caribbean* trilogy) and a critically-acclaimed performance as Sweeney Todd, Depp has Hollywood in the palm of his hand. Having wilfully bucked the establishment throughout his entire career, he has somehow managed to conquer both realms of acting and is regarded as a serious, respected actor as well as a bankable movie star.

Many attribute Depp's somewhat belated box-office success and the accompanying long overdue Academy Award nominations to the happiness brought to him by family life. Since 1998, he has been with French actress, singer and model, Vanessa Paradis. The couple, who divide their time between homes in Paris, the South

Vanessa, Lily-Rose and Jack have brought me great happiness. For me, they are the key to success.

of France, Los Angeles and a deserted island in the Bahamas, have two children: a daughter, Lily-Rose, and a son, Jack. Depp speaks often of the joy of family life and how it has healed something inside him and taught him a peace of mind he never knew before. He recently revealed, "Before my children came along, I didn't know that family was the most wonderful, moving thing in the world. Vanessa, Lily-Rose and Jack have brought me

ABOVE: Johnny with soulmate Vanessa Paradis, his partner since 1998. The couple have two children.

great happiness. For me, they are the key to success." And with a slew of other fascinating roles in the pipeline, it would seem that his appeal is here to stay.

CHAPTER ONE

The

EARLY YEARS

ABOVE RIGHT: Johnny with his beloved mother Betty Sue. Her name is tattooed on his left arm.

On 9 June 1963 John Christopher Depp II was born in Owensboro, Kentucky. First settled in 1797, this small town on the southern banks of the Ohio was originally known as "Yellowbanks" on account of the yellow soil lining the banks of the river. John Depp Senior worked as a civil engineer while his mother, Betty Sue Palmer, was a waitress at a local coffee shop. This was their fourth, youngest and final child. Born a Gemini, John Depp II would later discover he shares a birthday with fellow actors Michael J. Fox, Natalie Portman and Jackie Mason, as well as jazz legend Cole Porter. The couple already had a son, Danny, and two daughters, Christie and Debbie. Like them, John inherited a unique mix of Cherokee, German and Irish blood. To differentiate from his father, early on in his life the family took to calling him "Johnny".

The family lived on a meagre income and Depp would later describe his upbringing as "poor". Apparently his earliest childhood memory was of catching lightning bugs, creatures he found both fascinating and beautiful. With his older siblings, he quickly acquired a slew of nicknames such as "Johnny Dip", "Deppity Dog" and "Dippity Do". As a child, he was especially close to one of his grandfathers, who he called "Paw Paw". Another early memory for him was of picking tobacco in Kentucky with Paw Paw. He has spoken of being "inseparable" from his grandfather and not surprisingly, when Paw Paw died, he was devastated. Already a firm believer in ghosts, the seven-year-old dealt with his grandfather's death from a supernatural point of view. When Paw Paw died, he began to sense his presence and for him, this feeling of his grandfather's spirit being occasionally present has continued ever since, his force felt most strongly during times of crisis.

Soon after Paw Paw's death, the Depp family left Owensboro for a new life in Florida. The move paved the way to an era of instability and uncertainty. When they first reached Florida, they lived in a succession of motels while John Depp Senior and Betty Sue looked for work. Soon they were employed once more as civil engineer and waitress, and left their transient life behind them and settled into a house. Of the various addresses that followed during this time of upheaval and change, Depp has often talked of one specific home on the corner of a busy street in Miramar, Florida. Built in the 1960s the house had three bedrooms. He shared a room with his brother, Danny, who was always blasting out Van Morrison and Bob Dylan. Depp has strong memories of Danny and his sister Christie fighting; also his mother's cooking smells flooding the house – soup, beans and ham, in particular – and fond times with his pet poodle Pepi.

He has said that by the time he was fifteen the family had lived in approximately twenty different houses. Naturally, the constant moving took its toll and to this day, he says that whenever he packs a suitcase, it triggers old childhood anxieties. To deal with the lack of stability, while still a boy, Depp developed a fantasy world into which he could escape. For instance, he and a friend would make covert tape recordings of people talking and they would also dig deep tunnels in the backyard. To keep these tunnels a secret, they covered the holes with wooden boards or heaps of leaves. His ultimate plan was to dig a tunnel from the backyard to his bedroom, creating a perfect escape route. At this time, he was also fascinated with the stuntman Evil Knievel and by the Second World War (hence the digging of tunnels). Evil Knievel represented a recklessness and danger that seems to have always intrigued him. Later, he would be equally in awe of other daredevil individuals, such as the writer Hunter S. Thompson and Rolling Stones guitarist, Keith Richards.

Depp continues to have a strong belief in the realm of the supernatural. Often he has spoken of being plagued by strange dreams and daydreams as a child and of having intense dreams in which, while definitely awake, he was struck dumb and a face would appear. He was convinced the faces were restless spirits trying to communicate secrets they unwillingly took to the grave.

At school in Miramar, Depp felt isolated and alienated. He was singled out as an outsider and picked on by a group of kids. To add to the problem, one teacher in particular directed her hostile attentions towards him. Despite this, he made a select handful of good friends that in turn, brought on another sort of hurt: whenever they invited him over to their homes after school, he saw a different kind of family life. Up to this point, he assumed he had a regular upbringing. For instance, he'd go to a friend's house and the family would sit down to dinner, something that rarely happened in his own home. Depp has said that his family didn't sit down to dinner together. Instead, he would grab a sandwich and then go out or up to his room. Everyone would eat separately. At one friend's house, the family sat down to a dinner that included romaine lettuce. Johnny thought it was weird: he'd never seen it before. Other families served soup, appetizers, salad… again, all foreign to him. Having grown up, as he has said, on "hillbilly food", the idea of sitting down as a family to a wholesome nutritious three-course dinner seemed completely bizarre to him.

Although Depp has always maintained that his parents did the best they could for him and his siblings, at this point in his life it began to dawn on him that his family had its problems. The six of them lived in a small house and there were frequent explosive arguments. By the time he was twelve, he had grown out of his boyhood obsessions and discovered rock'n'roll, mostly through his older brother's love of music. He became a big fan of the band, Kiss, known for their costume, make-up and loud guitars. In a bid to emulate an onstage stunt by the band's frontman Gene Simmons, Johnny nearly scarred himself for life. He and a friend placed a T-shirt on the end of a broom handle. Next, they doused the shirt in gasoline and lit it. Johnny then put gasoline in his mouth and, in an attempt to emulate Simmons, tried to breathe out a trail of fire. But the stunt backfired and for a split second his face roared up in flames. That evening, to prevent his mother from knowing what happened, he told her that his face (temporarily, but superficially burned) had been injured in a fireworks' accident.

Depp's interest in rock'n'roll arrived hand in hand with an early teenage rebellion, no doubt exaggerated by the difficult atmosphere at home and years of moving from one place to another. Also, at the same age, he managed to get himself suspended from school for a fortnight by flashing the teacher that he felt was constantly picking on him. The teacher, a woman, tended to ridicule Johnny and single him out in class. He felt she was unfair, even brutal and that she had elected him as the focal point for all her spite and loathing. One day in class it seemed to him that she was trying particularly hard to embarrass him in front of his schoolmates. So he got up, crossed the room and headed for the door. Just before leaving the room, he dropped his trousers and mooned her. The teacher was furious and had Johnny appear in the Dean's office. As a result of this stunt, he was suspended.

As so often happens, the suspension set Johnny off on a wave of bad behaviour that snowballed. Deemed a troublemaker at school, he wore the label well. He and his friends got into scrapes typical of boys their age. Depp later recalled, "I experimented with drugs and I experimented with everything that little boys do – vandalism, throwing eggs at cars, breaking and entering schools and destroying a room." Overnight it seemed that his powerful imagination and inner fantasy world exploded outwards into behaviour expressive of his inner turmoil. He was no longer content to dig tunnels, read about the Nazis, record people talking or read books on Evil Knievel. Instead he listened to Kiss, discovered drugs, played up at school and roamed wild about the local neighbourhood, getting up to no good.

Against this backdrop of mischief and rebellion, Johnny was given a positive outlet for his frustration when his mother bought him an electric guitar for $25. Throughout his childhood he had been exposed to live music and instruments by an uncle – a Baptist minister – whose family had a gospel group. Watching

ABOVE: Kiss were one of Johnny's favourite bands when he was in his early teens.

his uncle's group play live inspired Johnny to learn to play guitar. When his mother bought him the guitar, it was an epiphany for the twelve-year-old. Suddenly, he had a purpose, a goal, ambition. He wanted to become a legendary guitar player, to form a great band and make it as a rock star. Although he didn't sign up for guitar lessons (probably because of the expense), he learned to play guitar by jamming along to his favourite records like Aerosmith's "Season of Wither" or albums by Alice Cooper and Kiss.

When Johnny was thirteen he formed the first of many bands and they called themselves Flame. Being in a band and playing guitar gave him a place in life. Finally, he felt as if he belonged somewhere. All his friends were fellow music fans, interested in learning an instrument and playing in a band. With the band came a more flamboyant personal image. Depp wore plain T-shirts and clothes stolen from his mother's wardrobe – crushed velvet shirts, bellbottoms. Having set his sights on rock stardom, his schoolwork suffered, but he made no pretence of being interested. Instead he grew his hair long and stayed away from all school activities. He'd take his guitar into school but skip regular classes and go to the music practice room where he'd sit, mastering the instrument.

Johnny's next obsession was Peter Frampton's seminal multi-million selling 70s double live album, *Frampton Comes Alive*. This lasted until his brother Danny turned him on to a whole new array of music. It started when he heard Van Morrison's *Astral Weeks* humming through the wall of his brother's bedroom. Instantly struck by this other kind of music, he dedicated himself to travelling his brother's record collection, listening to everything from soundtrack albums like *A Clockwork Orange* and *Last Tango In Paris* to Bob Dylan albums to classical works by composers such as Brahms and Mozart.

While still thirteen, Johnny started playing club shows with Flame. He loved the adrenaline rush and energy of playing live rock'n'roll on stage. Like Tommy Stinson, bassist of a band he would later love – The Replacements – who started playing clubs when he was twelve, Johnny almost certainly faked his ID to fool promoters and club managers, finding himself a pretender in an adult world. Playing at being grown-up, he grew up fast. He lost his virginity to a girl who hung around the band. She was slightly older and, according to Johnny, also a virgin. They first slept together in the blue Ford van that belonged to the bassist in Flame. For a short while after, Johnny and this girl dated, but the relationship never

RIGHT: Rebel rockers like Alice Cooper made Johnny want to become a rock 'n' roll star.

Tommy Stinson, bassist of a band he would later love 'The Replacements' who started playing clubs when he was twelve

really got off the ground and they soon lost touch. Meantime, he and his adolescent friends ran wild. They experimented with drugs, broke into school and trashed rooms, got into fights, got drunk regularly, smoked cigarettes and engaged in petty episodes of shoplifting. Depp has claimed that by the age of fourteen he had done "every kind of drug there was".

Within this chaos he also began to cut himself to mark significant events in his life. It started when he carved his initials on his arm and soon became a habit that he apparently stopped in his twenties. Depp has since rationalized his actions, telling *Details* magazine in 1993 that he always viewed his body as a journal and that the scars from the cutting are intense diary entries, reminding him of the mood or events of a particular time. He has never spelled out whether

ABOVE: Tommy Stinson of the Replacements performing at I Beam, San Francisco in 1985.

the cutting was ritualistic body scarring (tribal and ceremonial in its nature to the same effect as his many tattoos) or an act of self-harm (a common symptom of psychological turmoil and emotional disturbance).

But he eventually realized he was on a slippery slope of ever-more destructive behaviour, one that could ruin his life if he didn't do something about it. (These periods of bingeing on bad behaviour and then pulling back from the edge would later develop into something of a pattern in Depp's life. While filming *What's Eating Gilbert Grape* he would similarly spiral near out of control and then pull an identical U-turn.) This time the catalyst for change came when

ABOVE: Jack Kerouac, his book *On the Road* changed
and shaped Depp's life for good.

he realized that the kids around him who were doing
drugs, drinking and flunking at school were heading
nowhere fast. Seeing in their downward spiral a flash of
what could happen to him if he didn't change course,
he pulled back from the edge and cut the cord on the
self-destructive impulses propelling his recent life.

Just as his rebellious streak was cooling off,
Johnny's parents announced they were getting
divorced. Though hardly a surprise the news still hit
him hard: it was the biggest blow since Paw Paw's
passing away. After the split he went to live with
his mother, Betty Sue. She was very upset over the
divorce and he took on the responsibility of taking
care of her. He later said that his own feelings about
the divorce, his own hurt, his own pain, was secondary
at the time to helping his mother feel better.

Around this time Danny lent Johnny a copy of
Jack Kerouac's *On the Road*, a book that was to change
his life and shape his future. He later said that for
him it became like "a Koran" such was its instructive
usefulness and impact. Up to this point he had read
little and now here was a book that seemed to speak
directly to him, telling him of a life beyond the only
reality he knew. The words, the breathless pace, the
story of American drop-outs on a road trip across
America in search of wisdom and experience captured
his imagination in the same way that *Astral Weeks*
mesmerised him when he was thirteen. He knew
right away that he wanted the world and life of *On the
Road* and not the predictable nine to five facing him in
Miramar, Florida. By the time he finished reading it, he
was already thinking of dropping out of high school.
Through reading other books by and about Kerouac,
Johnny discovered Kerouac's peers: other "Beat" writers
such as Gregory Corso, William S. Burroughs, Herbert
Huncke, Neal Cassady and Allen Ginsberg. Looking
back, he said of these discoveries: "I had found the
teachers and the proper motivation for my life."

Buoyed up and guided by these outsider voices
Johnny dropped out of high school as soon as he turned
sixteen in 1979. His plan was to throw everything into
trying to make it as a rock star. He moved out of his
mother's house and took a job as a pump attendant at a
gas station. At this point, having already played in many
different bands, he joined a new band called The Kids
and played a 1956 cream Fender Telecaster guitar, his
rhythmic, straightforward technique inspired by Keith
Richards. Meanwhile he had found a serious girlfriend:
Lori Ann Allison. Her brother played drums for The
Kids. Through him the couple met and hit it off. Lori
was five years older than him, not that this mattered
to either of them. Soon they were dating and in love.

The Kids, who Johnny later described as a cross
between U2 and The Sex Pistols, initially played sets
covering old songs. Once established they started to
incorporate original material into their sets. By the
turn of 1980 they'd built up a loyal local following
and opened for major acts passing through Florida,
such as The B-52s, A Flock of Seagulls, The Pretenders
and Talking Heads. Famously, in 1981, they opened

for Iggy Pop. But meeting a hero was too much for Johnny. He didn't know how to behave and so he got drunk. Unfortunately, he overdid it and ended up screaming insults at Iggy, who was not amused and called him "a little turd". (Later on when they worked together on John Water's *Cry-Baby* they would become friends and laugh about the incident.)

With his family splintered and the structure of school now history, Johnny must have felt a deep need for some security and stability in his life. This was surely on his mind when he proposed to Lori Ann. Not even out of his teens, he was rushing into marriage. Too young to understand the implications, he was surely looking to heal the pain of his parents' divorce. On many occasions Depp has also said that he has a very traditional attitude to getting married and having kids. Undoubtedly acting out of these values, Johnny put the question to Lori Ann and she said yes.

Figuring they would never make it if they stayed in Florida, on the advice of Don Ray, the booker at the Palace club in Hollywood, The Kids decided to head west in search of a record label. Ray, who was interested in managing the band, suggested they move out to Los Angeles. He advanced the band some expenses that partly covered their relocation expenses. To this they pooled their collective savings and drove all the way from Florida to California. Arriving, they changed their name to Six Gun Method. Though convinced the move would net them their dream record deal, disillusion quickly set in. Having been modestly successful on the local circuit in Florida, in Los Angeles they found themselves back at the bottom of the ladder. Once more they were just another struggling rock band looking for a lucky break.

To make ends meet, Johnny took a succession of pay-the-rent jobs. He did time as a construction labourer, a mechanic and a screen printer while Lori Ann, who had made the move out to Los Angeles to be with him and the band, found work as a make-up artist. Despite the lack of breaks and the accompanying financial struggles, on 20

RIGHT: In 1981 Johnny's band opened for Iggy Pop, but meeting his hero proved too much and ended in disaster.

'I had found the teachers and the proper motivation for my life'

ABOVE: Lori Ann Allison, Johnny's first love and wife. The couple divorced in 1985.

December 1983 Johnny married Lori Ann. Feeling a traditional need to support his wife, he found regular work as a telemarketer selling ballpoint pens over the phone and was paid $100 a week.

Time went by and still the band remained stuck in a rut, opening for artists like Billy Idol, just as they had in Florida. The pressure of the band not working out got to Johnny and he became frustrated. Money was a constant source of anxiety and he hated his

LEFT: Early on in life, Johnny was happiest on stage playing electric guitar.

day job. Lori Ann was still working as a make-up artist. Both grew tired of trying to make the rent. They did some growing up and realized they weren't working as a couple. Inevitably, the marriage broke up. Later Depp, who has kept very tight-lipped about the marriage and the reasons for its failure, said: "I was married when I was twenty. It was a strong bond with someone but I can't necessarily say I was in love." The couple decided to separate but remained close friends, which suggests the split was a mutual decision. But their divorce would not be finalized until 1985. In the meantime, Lori Ann would make an introduction that was to change the course of Johnny's life in ways he would never have expected.

LEFT: With his band The Kids, Johnny left Florida for Los Angeles in search of fame.

CHAPTER TWO

SLOW BURN

ABOVE RIGHT: Johnny in his auspicious film debut, *A Nightmare On Elm Street*.

Having parted on amicable terms, Lori Ann and Johnny stayed in touch. Desperately wanting to help her soon-to-be ex-husband find a path in life that would make him happy, Lori Ann introduced him to a young actor she had befriended through her work. The actor was Nicolas Cage, who was emerging due to his acclaimed performance in *Rumblefish* (1983). At the time Johnny was flat broke. He and Cage got along well and on hearing about his rock dreams, Cage asked him if he'd ever considered acting. Johnny told him that beyond being a James Dean fan, he hadn't. Sensing a hidden talent Cage recommended he meet an agent that he knew.

Although he agreed to meet the agent (Tracey Jacobs), Johnny had no intention of sacrificing his love of music. Instead, he was thinking that acting might be a smart way to bankroll the band. He could take a variety of acting jobs, put away the cash and then return to his rock'n'roll ambitions without feeling he had a gun to his head when it came to paying the rent and putting food on the table. Impressed and seeing the logic in Cage's matchmaking, much to Johnny's surprise Jacobs signed the unknown to her roster despite his lack of acting background or experience.

The first thing Jacobs did was to send Johnny to an audition for a part in a new film by horror director Wes Craven. The character he would be reading for was a typical blond-haired, football-loving jock. Johnny doubted he'd be right for the part. He turned up to the reading with spiky hair and earrings, looking (in his own words) like "a little fucking catacomb dweller". But, having rehearsed the lines around the clock in preparation, he shone at the audition. "He just had a very powerful and yet subtle personality," said Craven of the unknown budding actor's reading for the part. "There was some sort of charisma about him. My teenage daughter and her friend were there at the reading and they absolutely flipped out over him – he's got real sex appeal for women."

Hours later Johnny received a call from Jacobs, who quite simply informed him: "You're an actor." To his amazement he had landed the part of Glen Lantz, the boyfriend. The film would turn out to be *A Nightmare On Elm Street*, a hugely successful horror movie that would gross $25 million when it opened across the USA in November 1984 and

ABOVE and RIGHT: Johnny in teen sex comedy *Private Resort*.

spawn multiple sequels. After six years of sweating with different bands and getting all but nowhere, the instant success was hard to compute. No one, least of all Johnny, could have expected such an overnight change in fortunes. For the six weeks he worked on the film he was paid $1,500 a week, more money than he'd ever seen before. Throwing himself into this new career opening, he read up on acting legends such as Stanislavski, the godfather of Method acting.

Despite his new enthusiasm for acting, other parts were less than forthcoming. Keen to continue making the large sums of money he'd earned on *A Nightmare On Elm Street*, Johnny accepted any part that came his way – a far cry from the discerning, idiosyncratic choice of roles that would later form part of his trademark as an actor. The first of these was a part in a short student film called *Dummies*, directed by Laurie Frank, a student at the AFI (American Film Institute). He was cast opposite a young, upcoming actress called

Sherilyn Fenn. Born 1 February 1965, Fenn had so far only appeared only in Art Linson's teenage comedy *The Wild Life* (released in 1984) and a made-for-TV film called *Silence of the Heart* (also released in 1984).

During the three-day shoot, Johnny and Fenn got along extremely well and started dating. He was twenty-two, Fenn seventeen. They fell madly in love and soon after Johnny apparently moved in with the budding actress. Around the clock both pursued further acting breaks. They were in the same position – trying to make it, each with a few promising credits to their name.

In the same spirit of "take any role that paid and got him working", Johnny's next role was that of "Jack" in a disposable teen movie called *Private Resort*. Directed by George Bowers and co-starring Rob Morrow, it was about two teenage boys who spend a weekend at a Florida resort in pursuit of girls. Unsurprisingly, when the film was released in 1985, it vanished without trace. Still desperate for

any work, for his third role Johnny played a small part in a made-for-TV movie called *Slow Burn* (1986), directed by Matthew Chapman. The lacklustre, formulaic thriller, starring Eric Roberts and Beverly D'Angelo, saw Johnny take on the role of "Donnie", a millionaire's son in a story about a man who hires a private investigator to find his ex-wife and son ("Donnie"). Of this and *Private Resort*, Depp later said, "I made some shitty movies when I was first starting out, but I'm not embarrassed by them, especially as I didn't think I was going to be an actor. I was trying to make some money – I was still a musician."

In a bid to get more serious about acting and break out of the "light" roles in which *A Nightmare On Elm Street* had predictably typecast him, Johnny enrolled for acting classes at The Loft Studio in Los Angeles, hoping to learn more about the craft. Former student Nicolas Cage recommended the Studio to him. But Johnny had barely started classes when Tracey Jacobs called in January 1986 to say that she wanted him to read for a part in a Vietnam War movie, *Platoon* (1986), written and directed by Oliver Stone. He read the script and loved it then Jacobs had him meet Stone. The director was so impressed he called Jacobs the same day and offered Johnny the part of "Lerner". That summer he set off for the Philippines, leaving Fenn behind. He joined the rest of the cast in a vigorous training programme in the jungle to lend the platoon a vital authenticity. Missing Fenn, he scrawled her name across his character's helmet, a detail that helped him bring "Lerner" to life as a character. Close observers can spot this in the finished film.

Back from the Philippines, no other acting jobs came up. With Six Gun Method now history, Johnny hooked up with another Florida band recently relocated to Los Angeles called Rock City Angels. A Glam Rock/70s Rock outfit, Rock City Angels sported a Keith Richards' image: messed-up hair, leather, make-up and guitars. They started out in Florida as The Abusers before renaming themselves Rock City Angels. On the Florida circuit they had crossed paths with The Flame

ABOVE: Actress Sherilyn Fenn, later of *Twin Peaks* fame, with whom Johnny fell in love while making a short film.

and The Kids. In Los Angeles they fitted right in with the music scene of the time. Guns N' Roses had signed to Geffen and were on the brink of massive success. Their leap to stardom left a gaping hole in the club circuit and promoters were thankful to find Rock City Angels waiting in the wings. In late 1985 the band underwent a personnel change, leaving them short of a guitarist. When they ran into Johnny in Los Angeles, he was an obvious replacement. The band was tipped for big things and had a solid fan base. Once more,

it seemed he had reverted to his first love: music.

Late in 1986 Tracey Jacobs received a call from Fox requesting that Johnny audition for the starring role of Officer Tom Hanson in a new TV show called *Jump Street Chapel*. The show would revolve around a group of undercover police officers young enough to pose as high school students in order to

BELOW: After appearing in *Platoon*, Johnny joined Rock City Angels on guitar, reverting to his first love.

Once more, it seemed he had reverted to his first love: music

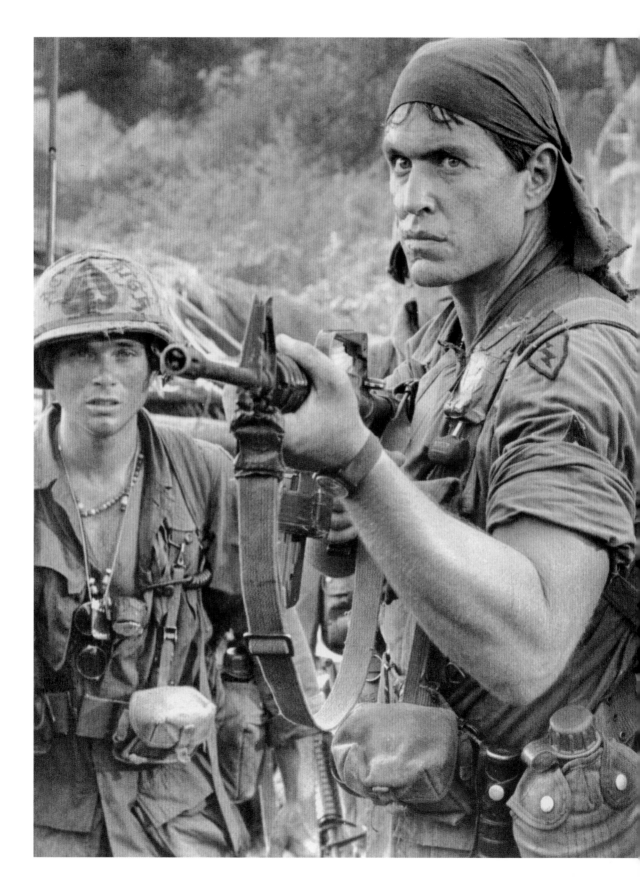

LEFT: Johnny in Oliver Stone's *Platoon*. Much of his role ended up on the editing-room floor.

bust criminals operating in the realm of teenagers. Fresh from the seriousness of working on set with Oliver Stone and busy playing guitar for Rock City Angels, Johnny told his agent he wasn't interested in looking at the script for the Teen Cop drama. He was wary of becoming signed up to a TV show that might run for years and prove stifling for his career.

The part went to Jeff Yagher, who left three weeks into filming, and so the producers thought of Johnny again. By now he had learned that many of his substantial scenes in *Platoon* had been cut in the editing room, leaving his character with a minor role. Hearing this news and having been evicted from his apartment, he was ready to reconsider. Staying at a friend's apartment and still struggling to pay off a stack of bills, he read for the part. He impressed the supervising producer, Steve Beers, who said of the reading: "He was laid-back, he had this presence." Fox offered Johnny the role and he signed up for the show, figuring it wouldn't be a long-term commitment. He was under the impression that his involvement with the show would last a maximum of a year. That, he figured, he could deal with.

Unable to commit to both the TV show and Rock City Angels, Johnny had to quit the band. Months later Geffen Records, sensing a new potentially lucrative audience for the Glam Rock/Hard Rock sound of Guns N' Roses, signed Rock City Angels for the then unheard-of sum of $6.2 million. Johnny must have wondered if he'd made the right decision. But two years later Geffen dropped the band and by then Johnny Depp was a massive star.

CHAPTER THREE

21 JUMP STREET

ABOVE RIGHT: TV series *21 Jump Street* quickly turned Johnny into a pin-up.

Just as the deal was signed *Platoon* opened that December at a select handful of cinemas in the USA, allowing for a word-of-mouth buzz to build. It went on general release in February 1987, by which time the film had become both a critical and commercial hit. Johnny's star was in ascension: *A Nightmare On Elm Street*, *Platoon* and now a hit TV show was waiting around the corner.

Renaming the show *21 Jump Street* (the earlier title was a reference to the district police station where the officers were based, being a converted church), Fox rushed Johnny to Vancouver, British Columbia, where the show was filmed. The first task was to re-shoot the pilot episode with Johnny in Yagher's place. Needing to relocate from Los Angeles, Johnny talked his mother into temporarily moving there with him. Next, he tried to persuade Sherilyn Fenn to join him. But Fenn was not in a position to leave Los Angeles and the Hollywood circuit. She needed to be there for auditions and meetings, not to mention the various films in which she was appearing. Consequently she and Johnny took turns to travel back and forth between Vancouver

'Historically, when a show becomes really popular, actors turn into giant assholes, but not Johnny.'

and Los Angeles. On one such trip Fenn made a guest appearance in the ninth episode of the show.

Playing up his good looks and pin-up potential, the publicists at Fox began talking Johnny up with editors at teen magazines. But Johnny was not expecting all the focus to be on him as the star of the show with a heavy emphasis on marketing his good looks. He felt concerned that he was being turned into a product, a face to sell. His background of admiring outlaws, outsiders, and outcasts didn't sit well with this feeling.

When the pilot debuted on the Fox Network on 21 April 1987 Johnny was thrust into overnight success and turned into a teen idol and pin-up for millions of adoring female fans. He also received a pay cheque of $45,000 per episode, an incredible amount of money for a twenty-four-year-old actor, who had been struggling to pay the rent just months earlier. Estranged from his life in Los Angeles, working fifteen-hour days, spending most of the remaining nine asleep or learning lines and now an overnight TV star, he struggled to get his head around all the changes. Perhaps as a way to ground him, around this time Johnny proposed to Fenn and the actress said yes. Once more he was engaged, thinking of getting married, settling down. For a pin-up, this was a contrary scenario. To Johnny's adoring female fans, it made him unattainable and unavailable, but it also showed him to be a committed boyfriend. If anything, it probably boosted his desirability.

The show dealt with topical issues and as a result, attracted a loyal, young following. In the first episode, Johnny (as Officer Tom Hanson) gets posted to Jump Street because a group of criminals he was trying to arrest didn't take him seriously, thinking he was too young to be a police officer. Transferred, Hanson goes undercover to bring down a high school drug dealer. In the second episode, he goes undercover to bust a group of high school kids stealing cars and in the third, again undercover, he busts those responsible for a string of burglaries at high schools. This was typical of the show's plot lines. Juvenile crime, in its various guises, was always the subject. Hanson and his colleagues

LEFT: Initially the role of Tom Hanson brought Johnny fame, money and stability.

were always assigned to bust the perpetrators.

The show became an instant success with young viewers, so much so that Fox set up a telephone help-line so viewers could call in after the show to discuss whatever pertinent issues that particular episode had raised. Typical subjects, as outlined above, also included teenage pregnancy, domestic abuse and peer pressure. Because of the moral focus of the show and the way adult issues were applied to a high-school context, Johnny found himself on the receiving end of an ever-swelling mailbag. The letters mostly came from high-school students, many addressed and written to "Tom Hanson", such was the chord his character struck with those still at school. Just as many, of course, were declarations of love and lust from female admirers. At the peak of his involvement with the show, he was receiving an average of ten thousand fan letters a month. Some were from girls threatening to commit suicide if he didn't write back. Fearing for their wellbeing and understanding their dark moods, Johnny always replied.

Having persuaded his mother, now remarried, to join him in Vancouver when the show originally started shooting, it turned out she and her new husband actually liked it better than Florida and moved there permanently. His father, though, was still back in Florida, where he was now director of public works and utilities for the city of Hallendale.

Recognizing that the show had millions of impressionable young viewers, Fox started to have Johnny shoot public service announcements, which were tacked on to the end of certain shows. Or they simply advertised help-lines relating to the subject covered in an episode. For instance, when they did a show in which a teenager was in trouble with drugs, they ran a drug-abuse hotline at the end of the show and were inundated with a huge number of calls from viewers. Helping kids going through the same kind of turbulent adolescence that he went through made Johnny feel good.

To deal with the pressure of fame, he got into a habit of letting off steam by goofing about on set. His co-workers were impressed that he had a sense of humour about his overnight fame. Patrick Hasburgh,

ABOVE: Being pigeon-holed as a teen pin-up soon started to frustrate Johnny.

the creator of *21 Jump Street*, said of one such typical incident: "Historically, when a show becomes really popular, actors turn into giant assholes, but not Johnny. He once lit his underwear on fire in the middle of the set but that was because no one had cleaned up his motor home in a long time. The show's success may prevent Johnny from taking features offers, but he's being cool about it, cooler than I'd be in his shoes. And if I were his age and looked like he does, I'd be dead by now. Girls follow him everywhere, screaming."

By early 1988, Johnny had broken up with Sherilyn Fenn. According to speculation (neither Johnny nor Fenn has ever discussed the relationship or why it failed in public), the relationship was brought down by the pressures of a long distance relationship. With Depp in Vancouver most of the time and Fenn in Los Angeles, not to mention their combined workloads, they had little quality time together, a long-term predicament that is believed to have caused them to drift. Living apart most of the time, the strain was eventually too much. Depp had also become a celebrity. Fenn, though acting in films like *Just One of the Guys* (1985), *Out of Control* (1985), *Thrashin'* (1986) and *The Wraith* (1986), was yet to hit the same level of notoriety. It would come for her a year later, in 1989, when she landed the part of "Audrey Horne" in David Lynch's hugely successful TV show *Twin Peaks*. Speculation also suggests that the different paces of their careers might have caused friction in the relationship, considering that when the couple first met, they were in the same position.

Soon after breaking up with Fenn, Johnny met

and fell in love with another actress: Jennifer Grey. Grey, who was born 26 March 1960 in New York, had appeared in *The Cotton Club* (1984) and *Ferris Bueller's Day Off* (1986) before shooting to fame in 1987 as the female star of *Dirty Dancing*. Three years older than Johnny, the twenty-eight-year-old actress knew exactly how he felt, having also been thrust into celebrity overnight. Both Depp and Grey have been infamously tight-lipped about their brief relationship, which lasted from 1988 until 1989. They are believed to have been engaged for the majority of their time together (the relationship lasted a total of eight months). Unlike Depp's later relationships

BELOW: After breaking up with Sherilyn Fenn, Johnny started dating *Dirty Dancing* star Jennifer Grey.

with Winona Ryder, Kate Moss and Vanessa Paradis, all of which were, or continue to be, lived out in the public eye, under intense media scrutiny, his earlier relationships are mostly veiled in privacy. Even with Johnny riding high in *21 Jump Street* and Grey a Star Du Jour on the back of *Dirty Dancing*'s runaway success, there is surprisingly little information to be found on how they met, what the attraction was or how quickly Johnny proposed. All that can be concluded is that they fell in love quickly and Johnny proposed equally fast, based on the short time frame of their relationship.

At work, Johnny was increasingly disgruntled with being marketed and pigeon-holed as a teen pin-up and idol, adored more for his looks than his acting ability. Sick of the situation and wanting to be taken

ABOVE: Three years older than Depp, Jennifer Grey knew all about the pressures of celebrity.

RIGHT: While she was still with Depp, Grey (right) filmed *Bloodhounds of Broadway* with Madonna (left).

seriously as an actor, he began to publicly express his frustration with the show. In late 1988, he said of his pin-up status, "I don't want to make a career of taking my shirt off. I'd like to shave off all my hair, even my eyebrows, try it that way. I don't fault the TV stars who do teen magazines. They took a hold of their situations, took offers that gave them the big money fast but they were dead in two years. I don't want that."

To deal with feeling so trapped (something every Gemini hates above all else), Johnny harboured dreams of one day directing a film or recording an album. On set, he provocatively altered and improvised his lines, departing from the script, much to the chagrin of the producers and writers. He played ever more practical jokes and pranks. The goofing around grew in proportion to his frustration. He felt stifled by the lack of creative possibilities. The formulaic nature of a TV show like *21 Jump Street* gave him little room to push his talents as an actor. As 1989 rolled in, he vowed he would get out of the show and pursue his own path as soon as he could.

In early 1989, Depp and Grey split up. Again speculation seems to suggest that the relationship faltered under the same strains as his romance with Fenn: that once again their combined work schedules left little time for the couple. With Johnny in Vancouver shooting *21 Jump Street* and Jennifer working on *Bloodhounds of Broadway* (1989), a vehicle for pop star Madonna, the couple were rarely in the same place at the same time. On top of this, he was going through a bad patch, feeling caged by his contractual ties to the TV show.

The break-up, his frustration with work and living in the public eye finally brought Johnny to breaking point while shooting the fourth season of *21 Jump Street* in Vancouver. After a day's shooting he went to a hotel to drop in on a friend who was staying there. To his surprise, the security guard on the door (who was new) wouldn't let him in saying it was too late for Johnny to come in unless he was a guest. Having been to the hotel many times, he allegedly got into a dispute with the guard. Apparently, an altercation followed and the police were called. Johnny was arrested and charged with "assault and mischief". All charges were later dropped.

The incident further fuelled his rebellious public image. In interviews promoting *21 Jump Street* he had been very candid about his teenage wild days of drinking and experimenting with drugs. Consequently, he was seen as a kind of James Dean figure, worshipped for his good looks but viewed as a bad boy outsider, a troubled trouble-maker. Girls loved him because he seemed mixed-up and in need of a good woman to take care of him. Maybe, they fantasized, I could be the one to straighten him out.

Meanwhile, various film scripts were being sent to his agent. To his disappointment, many of the roles were echoes of his part in *21 Jump Street*. But then salvation came in the form of a letter from director John Waters asking Johnny if he'd consider the lead role in a new film he was developing called *Cry-Baby* (1990). Johnny called Waters and they talked a little. "Johnny hated being a teen idol," recalled Waters at the time of the film's release. "And I told him the best way to get rid of an image, any image, is to make fun of it." Waters sent him a copy of the script and, when Johnny read for the part,

ABOVE: In many episodes of *21 Jump Street*, Johnny's character worked undercover, to bust drug dealers or gangs.

RIGHT: Despite the happy cast shot, Johnny was desperate to get out of his *21 Jump Street* contract.

he knew he'd found the actor to play "Wade": "He did this one little sneer in our first meeting, which summed it all up and I knew that, hey, Johnny Depp is Cry-Baby."

A spoof musical, *Cry-Baby* gave Johnny the chance to send up his past as a teenage hellraiser and his present typecast image as a teen pin-up. Set in Balitmore in 1954, the film charts the arrival of sex and drugs and rock'n'roll to the lives of a group of high-school kids as a sheltered girl falls for Wade

"Cry-Baby" Walker, a juvenile delinquent pretty boy from the wrong side of the tracks. The shoot started in spring 1989 and wrapped in summer when the fourth season of *21 Jump Street* aired on TV. The season, which ran through to 1990, was to be the last to feature Johnny. The final episode in which he appeared aired on TV in July 1990. But back in summer 1989 only one thing was on his mind: having Tracey Jacobs, his agent, get him out of the *21 Jump Street* contract.

CHAPTER FOUR

WINONA FOREVER

ABOVE RIGHT: Johnny's next big love was *Beetlejuice* star Winona Ryder.

In June 1989, at the première of *Great Balls Of Fire*, the biopic about the life and times of rock'n'roll legend Jerry Lee Lewis, Johnny locked eyes with the film's female star, Winona Ryder. The actress, who was born on 29 October 1971, was only seventeen at the time and best known for her performance in *Beetlejuice* (1988). In the lobby, as Ryder went to find herself a Coke, they exchanged glances. "It was a classic glance," Depp later said. "Like the lenses in *West Side Story* and everything else gets foggy." Ryder was equally struck: "It wasn't a long moment, but time seemed to be suspended." Although they didn't actually meet that night, Johnny said of their eyes locking, "I knew right then."

Several months later, in September 1989, a mutual friend took Winona to meet Johnny. He was staying at the Château Marmont hotel on Sunset Boulevard, on special location for an episode of *21 Jump Street*. Ryder was nervous: "I thought maybe he would be a jerk – I didn't know. But he was really, really shy." That evening they talked about their mutual affection for the books of J.D. Salinger, the soundtrack to the film *The Mission* and the music of Tom Waits and The Replacements. Finding they had so many things in common, Johnny asked Winona out on a date.

ABOVE: Johnny in his breakthrough role as loveable misfit Edward Scissorhands, with co-star and fiancée Winona Ryder.

so that in February 1990, five months after they started dating, Johnny gave Winona an engagement ring and the couple made their engagement public. Overnight media interest in the couple rocketed sky high and paparazzi started to tail their every move.

Meanwhile, Johnny had landed the lead role in Tim Burton's *Edward Scissorhands*. He would play the main character, "Edward Scissorhands", a fantasy of a boy with scissors for hands. Opposite Johnny, Winona would play Kim, a teenage girl trapped in a suburban nightmare. A romantic fairytale for outsiders, the role was perfect for Johnny. His teenage alienation and affection for outsiders gave him all the character background material he could possibly need. Rumours late in 1989 had initially suggested the lead role was going variously to Tom Cruise, Michael Jackson, William Hurt or Robert Downey Jr. Winona Ryder had been signed to the project since its earliest days, having always been Burton's first choice for "Kim". But Burton and Fox had struggled over which actor to cast as "Edward Scissorhands". The character, who Burton described as "both simple and complicated, both beautiful and off-putting, both creative and horrifically clumsy", would require the perfect actor or the film's magical elements would fail to come alive.

When Johnny saw the screenplay, he knew he had to get the part. He thought it was one of the best things he'd ever read in any form, such was his connection to Burton's creation. But when he read for the part, Burton knew nothing of his previous work, nor that the twenty-seven-year-old actor was engaged to Winona Ryder. During the meeting, however, he was impressed by Johnny's ability to "act with his eyes" but when he checked out his earlier work, including *21 Jump Street*, he worried that the public still saw Johnny Depp as "Tom Hanson", a persona who was the total antithesis of "Edward Scissorhands". Regardless, he followed his gut instinct and cast Johnny: "I knew right from the beginning that Johnny got it. Yes, he looks the way he looks but as a person he's much more like these other characters and that's what I love about him."

The meeting between Johnny Depp and Tim Burton was the beginning of both a close personal friendship and a close working relationship. In much the same way

She had hardly dated before, later famously telling a journalist, "I never really had a boyfriend before."

For their first date, they went to a party in the Hollywood Hills thrown by Ryder's godfather, counter-culture guru, Dr Timothy Leary. Having grown up in awe of outlaw personalities like Leary, Johnny was in seventh heaven. Here was a girl who belonged to this world – she hadn't needed to read *On the Road* to know about it. But if Winona had any doubts that she was simply the latest actress in Johnny's love life – there was even a bumper sticker famously doing the rounds at this time which read: 'Honk if you've never been engaged to Johnny Depp' – she took solace in knowing he was an old-fashioned romantic and only interested in monogamous relationships. As before, the relationship very quickly became intense and serious. So much

ABOVE: "Rebel teenager" Depp with co-star Amy Locane in the
film *Cry-Baby*.

as Robert De Niro's role as alter ego to Martin Scorsese,
Depp has become something of an alter ego for Burton.
Both share a dark, sensitive disposition and having
grown up in their imaginations, their connection was
intuitive and instant. Right from the start these two
exiled child-adults found they had much in common.

In February 1990 Johnny received his first award
for acting. In fact, it was a double whammy as both he
and Winona collected awards at the annual prestigious
ShoWest convention, the prominent movie industry
get together. Johnny won the "ShoWest Male Star of
Tomorrow" award, Winona the "ShoWest Female
Star of Tomorrow" award. They both went to Las
Vegas to receive the awards. The accolade confirmed
in his mind that he had a natural talent for acting,
not just for playing guitar in a rock'n'roll band.

In spring 1990, *Cry-Baby* opened at cinemas and
grossed $8 million in the USA. In interviews at the time,
Johnny opened up about his personal tastes. He said the
actors he most revered were Robert De Niro and Marlon
Brando. He revealed that his favourite music included
The Pogues, The Replacements, Frank Sinatra, Louis
Armstrong, The Clash, The Sex Pistols, Iggy Pop and
David Bowie and his preferred writers were Franz Kafka,
Jack Kerouac, J.D. Salinger and Charles Bukowski.

The actors he most revered were Robert De Niro and Marlon Brando

ABOVE and BELOW : John Waters's *Cry-Baby*, which opened just as filming started on *Edward Scissorhands*, gave Johnny the opportunity to send up the rebel teen image he was so keen to discard, and offered a taste of the much edgier roles to come.

As *Cry-Baby* opened, filming started on *Edward Scissorhands*. Feeling secure in his film projects, Johnny told his agent that he wanted out of *21 Jump Street*. Mid-shoot, she managed to remove him from his contract on a technicality. Johnny was delighted at the news. He felt free, out of a bind. Although he knew the show had made him, brought him money and fame, and put his career on the map, he swore he would never again pursue a commercial path for the sake of popularity or a pay-cheque. The show would roll on for a fifth and final season without Johnny, the last-ever episode screened on TV in 1991. "He made a choice when he came out of the television series," his agent said. "To take a left turn as opposed to right." The turn was a smart one. His work in *Edward Scissorhands* would end up earning Johnny a Golden

There's a sadness about Johnny I just respond to

ABOVE: Preparation for the role of Edward Scissor Hands was challenging as the character was unique.

BELOW: His performance in *Edward Scissorhands* showed that Johnny was about so much more than a hit TV show.

Globe nomination in the Best Performance by an Actor in a Motion Picture: Comedy/Musical category.

On the set of *Edward Scissorhands*, Johnny's co-stars were full of praise for what he did with the role. Diane Wiest, who plays Avon Lady Peg, was in awe: "People said he's a teen idol. I thought, 'Oh, great!' Then I met him. What a depth of talent! I'd look at him some days and I thought he's like Chaplin – he's got a walk and a sweetness of manner, he's just an angel." Winona, despite being in love with her co-star, was mesmerized by his performance: "Johnny played it like a little boy, which is a tough thing to do for an actor. Actors have this thing; they don't want to do anything to make them look innocent, naive, vulnerable. They all want to be macho, to carry a gun."

Johnny found preparation for the part a huge and

ABOVE: The boy with scissors for hands, who wanted to touch somebody but couldn't – these were feelings Depp could relate to.

BELOW: Winona Ryder on the set with *Edwards Scissorhands'* director Tim Burton.

exciting challenge. The character was completely unique, impossible to research. He saw "Edward Scissorhands" as having the innocence of a new-born or the unconditional loving affections of a dog. Burton later said that he believed Johnny had based the character of "Edward Scissorhands" on certain pets he'd had.

Tim Burton said that the seed for the other-worldly film was planted when he was going through adolescence. "I would go to clubs by myself and couldn't speak. It's rooted in depression, in having a lot of feelings inside that are very strong, and the very disturbing feeling of not being able to get those out to anybody." Out of those feelings, he imagined a boy with scissors for hands, "A fairytale visualization and physical outgrowth of wanting to touch somebody and not being able to." These were feelings Johnny could relate to. In Miramar, a high school outcast more interested in playing guitar than running with the pack, he had also experienced the chill of adolescent exile. Burton later concluded of Johnny's work on *Edward Scissorhands*: "He's more that character than anything else he's done. There's a sadness about Johnny I just respond to."

In May 1990, feeling the glare of constant media attention, Winona spoke of the pressures of two movie stars dating: "I don't even like discussing my relationship with Johnny with the press. It's nobody's business. How do you explain a relationship anyway? Nobody knows anything about it, nobody, not even friends know what my relationship is like. I don't even know it. You try to figure out your own feelings and interpret them for yourself, and you have these really strong, incredible, powerful feelings. And then some writer who doesn't know you at all is writing about it. It's like, Wait, what do you know?"

As a mark of his love for Ryder, Depp got a new tattoo on his arm at Sunset Strip Tattoo, which read "Winona Forever". "My previous relationships weren't as heavy as people think they were," he said of loving Ryder. "But there's never been anything throughout my twenty-seven years that's comparable to the feeling I have with Winona. You can think something is the real thing but it's different when you really feel it. The truth is very

powerful. Believe me, this 'Winona Forever' tattoo is not something I took lightly. Her eyes kill me."

Ryder was present when he got the tattoo, having never seen a tattoo made before. "I was sort of in shock," she said. "Besides, I'd never seen anyone get a tattoo before so I was pretty squeamish." For days afterwards she kept asking Johnny to lift the bandage and show her the tattoo. "I kept thinking it was going to wash off or something. I couldn't believe it was real. I mean it's a big thing because it's so permanent." Asked how she felt about such a powerful declaration of love, she said: "I was thrilled when he got the tattoo. Wouldn't any woman be?"

Late summer Johnny enjoyed the newfound freedom of not being committed to *21 Jump Street* for fifteen hours a day. He hung out with Winona. They were pursued everywhere by paparazzi. The couple were now dividing their time between two homes: a house in San Francisco and a loft that they'd bought in Manhattan. Although Winona said she wanted a New York base in order to escape from the excessive media hounding she was getting in Los Angeles, the media simply followed them to New York. In fact, as she and Johnny soon found out, they would follow them absolutely anywhere. She spoke in interviews of one particular incident that really bothered her: "Johnny and I flew into into LA from Tampa where we'd been working all day and we were really tired. We got off the plane and about fifty paparazzi people jumped out and started taking our pictures. We couldn't, like, see where we were going because the bulbs were popping. One guy stuck out his foot and tried to trip me. They were yelling at us, trying to get an interesting picture. Finally Johnny got so mad that he turned around and flipped them off. Now you'll see his picture in a magazine and he's going to look like some asshole."

For his next part, in early 1991, Johnny took a nostalgic cameo role in *Freddy's Dead: The Final Nightmare*, the latest instalment in the *A Nightmare on Elm Street* series. Although it contradicted his declaration that he was only going to work with the likes of Waters and Burton after leaving *21 Jump Street*, Johnny said he took the part as a way of paying his respects to Craven for giving him

ABOVE: Such was his love for her, Johnny got "Winona Forever" tattooed on his arm.

off. They were both constantly grilled on the subject of when their engagement would materialize into full-blown wedding plans. Winona told the press they'd get married when they had enough time out from work to take a long honeymoon. Johnny reiterated her point, telling reporters he wanted them to be able to get married, then go travelling for a few months. Little did they know their workload would never let up.

Johnny's next film project was determinedly left of centre. He took the role of "Axel Blackmar" in Emir Kusturica's new film, *Arizona Dream* because he had been a big fan of Kusturica's last film *Time of the Gypsies* (1988). For *Arizona Dream*, he would play a young man with a bleak future, who, having been orphaned at twenty after his parents die in a car crash, is offered a way out of his predicament by his Arizona-based Cadillac dealer uncle, played by Jerry Lewis.

Although Johnny was delighted to be working with a well-respected director and a cast that included Faye Dunaway, Lili Taylor and Vincent Gallo, the project was beset with mishaps. The first leg of filming took place in May and June of 1991, but then, because of financing problems, filming was put on hold. In the interim he revisited his rock roots, making a guest appearance in the promo video for Tom Petty's latest single "Into The Great Wide Open". By the time he was finished with that, Kusturica had resolved the financing problems and filming resumed and completed in 1992. But the problems didn't end there because the finished film was never released in the USA. Although it opened in France in January 1993 to critical acclaim, the project's ill-fated outcome meant Johnny had taken a significant step away from his affiliations with the mainstream success of *21 Jump Street*.

From *Arizona Dream*, he went to work on *Benny & Joon*, an offbeat love story starring Johnny as the eccentric character "Sam" and Mary Stuart Masterson as the mentally ill Juniper "Joon" Pearl. Aidan Quinn plays her brother (Benjamin "Benny" Pearl, who takes care of her). Initially, the film was slated to be a screwball comedy about two oddballs who fall in love, with Tom Hanks and Julia Roberts pencilled in for the "Sam" and "Joon" roles. Then Tim Robbins and Susan Sarandon were going to star, and then Johnny

his first break. In the end credits, his character is listed as "Oprah Noodlemantra". The film would open in September 1991 and cause no harm to Johnny's pursuit of respectability.

Meanwhile, the media's incessant intrusion upon his relationship with Winona was starting to take its toll. Johnny lashed out at the constant speculation that they had to live with. There were rumours that they were breaking up, that they were seeing other people, that they had broken up and that the engagement was

ABOVE: Johnny with Faye Dunaway in indie film *Arizona Dream*.

Depp and Laura Dern. Finally, director and studio agreed on Johnny, Masterson and Quinn. The director, Jeremiah Chechik, knew when he met Johnny that he was ideal for the role of Sam: "When I first met Johnny to discuss *Benny & Joon*, I began to understand how much he brought to the role of *Edward Scissorhands*. He is so emotionally expressive, doing what seems to be so little. It was clear that he would bring a thoroughly original and exciting energy to the role of Sam."

Filming began in July 1992. Because "Sam" is meant to be infatuated with Charlie Chaplin, Buster Keaton and Harold Lloyd, preparation for the role gave Johnny the chance to immerse himself in silent comedy. During the shoot he became very consumed in the character and turned in a performance that would earn him his second Golden Globe nomination in the Best Performance by an Actor in a Motion Picture: Comedy/Musical category.

Winona, meanwhile, had been shooting *Mermaids* (1990), *Night on Earth* (1991) and now *Dracula* (1992). Ushering in a case of déjà vu, they were apart a lot. These periods of separation put even more pressure on the couple, who were already bending under the strain of relentless media hounding. All too soon their romance would go the same way as Johnny's relationships with Fenn and Grey.

Taking a break from filming *Benny & Joon*, Johnny made another guest appearance in a promo video, this time The Lemonheads' single "It's A Shame About Ray".

When filming wrapped on *Benny & Joon*, Johnny went straight into research for his next part, that of "Gilbert Grape" in Lasse Halstrom's *What's Eating Gilbert Grape*. Following his work on *Edward Scissorhands*, *Arizona Dream* and *Benny & Joon*, this choice of role led many critics to speculate that he was deliberately seeking out left-field parts as part of an ongoing bid to erase all traces of the pin-up image that had dogged him so relentlessly since the first episode of *21 Jump Street* hit TV.

After seeing *Arizona Dream* Halstrom became interested in having Johnny read for "Gilbert Grape": "I found his performance subtle and honest," said the director. "The way he can convey sad emotions through his eyes. And working with him confirmed

ABOVE: The director of *Benny & Joon*, Jeremiah Chechik, knew Johnny was perfect for the role of Sam as soon as he met him.

what I saw in that movie. There's no way that you could force Johnny Depp to make a theatrical choice or a false choice. His choices always come from an inner place, from an emotional place that he can relate to."

He approached Johnny, in association with Peter Hedges, who adapted his own novel for the screenplay, when the film was still at seed stage. Hedges hadn't even finished the screenplay yet. Hearing what the role would entail and what the story was about, Johnny committed without hesitation. Hedges said of their first meeting, "He has almost a burning desire to

lead role of "Gilbert Grape" and newcomer Leonardo DiCaprio as "Arnie Grape", his kid brother. DiCaprio observed of the older actor, "He was extremely like Gilbert but it wasn't something Johnny was trying to do. It naturally came out of him. I never quite understood what he was going through because it wasn't some big emotional drama that was happening every day on the set. But subtle things I'd see in him would make me question what was going on. There's an element of Johnny that's extremely nice and extremely cool, but at the same time, he's hard to figure out. But that's what makes him interesting."

To play "Gilbert Grape", Johnny drew on his childhood in Florida and his days trapped on *21 Jump Street*. He said of the part: "I understand the feeling of being stuck in a place whether it's geographical or emotional. I can understand the rage of wanting to completely escape it and from everybody and everything you know and start a new life." To complete his portrait, he dyed his hair red and had his teeth bonded and then chipped out.

On set, Halstrom came to have a theory about Johnny's recent choice of roles: "It would have been easy to go at it in a cartoony way with these slightly grotesque characters. And I wanted them to seem authentic. Johnny's a very honest actor, but he likes to hide behind these oddball characters and I thought Gilbert would cut a little close to home." He was right. During filming, Johnny was in a place of personal turmoil. His relationship with Winona was on the rocks, fame was getting to him, the paparazzi wouldn't leave him alone. Seeking refuge from the successes of the past five years and having to live out his love life in public, he turned to drinking. Looking back on this era in 2004, he spoke to *Playboy* of his heavy drinking and use of other intoxicants: "There were drugs, too. Pills. And there was a danger that I would go over the edge. I could have, I thank God I didn't. It was darkest during the filming of *Gilbert Grape*."

Depp has spoken of self-medicating during this time, using alcohol and drugs to shut himself down. Inside there was turmoil and he needed to treat it. So he turned doctor and prescribed himself whatever shut down the discomfort and numbed the way he

make ugly choices. He comes with a physical beauty that's just astonishing and at the same time he has no interest in being that. When I met him he had this really long hair. He showed up at the meeting, very quiet, really shy and was teaching us magic tricks. I thought, I suppose he could be Gilbert."

Filming began in October 1992 with Johnny in the

ABOVE: Johnny with Mary Stuart Masterson in the offbeat romantic drama, *Benny & Joon*.

RIGHT: Johnny with co-stars Leonardo DiCaprio and Juliette Lewis in *What's Eating Gilbert Grape?*

was feeling. Some speculate that in choosing the role of "Gilbert Grape" he bit off more than he could chew. Not in terms of playing the role (his portrayal is excellent), but because of the emotional repercussions of being that character for a sustained period of time. Others speculate he was digesting a string of broken relationships, including the ailing present one with Ryder, all echoes of his parents' marriage breaking up.

All he wanted was to meet that one woman whom he loved and who loved him, who shared his traditional dream of marriage, kids, a nice little family. For a time he thought Winona Ryder was that woman – Lori Ann Allison, Sherilyn Fenn, Jennifer Grey, too. She was out there, of course, waiting in France – they just hadn't met yet.

When filming of *What's Eating Gilbert Grape* ended in January 1993, Johnny and Winona set about trying to fix the bends in their relationship.

However, Winona was going through her own parallel problems. Under pressure, like Johnny, from paparazzi, reporters and a busy work schedule, she had gone straight from *Dracula* to *The House of the Spirits* (1993), an adaptation of Isabel Allende's bestselling novel. Then, once work was finished, she voluntarily checked herself into a psychiatric hospital for five days, claiming to be suffering from sleep deprivation and insomnia. When she was discharged, she went straight to work on Martin Scorsese's *The Age of Innocence* (1993). She was drifting in a haze, in no state to help Johnny, who was in no condition to help her. Consequently both of them were alone together.

Meantime family and friends had expressed their concern to Johnny about his drinking. Although he took their concern seriously and pledged to cut back on his self-destructive behaviour, he didn't change his lifestyle. He appeased them but carried on. But then,

There's no way that you could force Johnny Depp to make a theatrical choice or a false choice. His choices always come from an inner place, from an emotional place that he can relate to.

'There's an element of Johnny that's extremely nice and extremely cool, but at the same time, he's hard to figure out. But that's what makes him interesting.' Leonardo DiCaprio

ABOVE: While filming *What's Eating Gilbert Grape?*, Johnny was going through a personal crisis off-set.

as had happened before when he was fifteen, he saw that he was walking perilously close to the edge. As in Miramar, he took a step back, pulled a U-turn, and made the decision to stop self-medicating. Later he said of this decision and its repercussions: "So I stopped everything for the better part of a year. I guess I just reached a point where I said, 'Jesus Christ, what am I doing? Life is fucking good! What am I doing to myself?'"

Johnny and Winona both knew their relationship was coming to an end. Ryder remembers neither wanted to do the breaking up. The decision to split up, though, was mutual. In one interview, she recalled driving around alone at night during this time, unable to sleep and seeing a billboard that said "Winona Ryder: The Luckiest Girl In The World". The irony of

such a statement was devastating. Finally, the couple put an end to their engagement. On 21 June 1993 they made the news public, declaring their relationship over. Although both blamed the media for the collapse of their relationship, in reality, they simply drifted apart. As with Fenn and Grey, Johnny and Winona were constantly working, always in different places, meeting where and whenever they could. Once again the strains of a long distance relationship were too much. On top of this, the media hounding put a lot of stress on their romance, rumours often getting to them: "We couldn't go a week without reading something that either wasn't true or was only half true, or was taken out of context," said Ryder after the break-up. "I wouldn't want to go through that again. Looking back, I can see that it did affect our relationship. I was at an age when I was really insecure."

Such was the extent of the media intrusion that

ABOVE: Co-star Juliette Lewis with Johnny Depp in a scene from *What's Eating Gilbert Grape*.

it took a lot of effort and plotting for Johnny and Winona to even arrange a quiet get-together without an audience of photographers. This subterfuge, perhaps fun at first, eventually became a drag. "It's very hard to have a personal life in this town," said Depp later on. "My relationship with Winona, it was my mistake to be as open as we were, but I thought if we were honest it would destroy that curiosity monster. Instead it fed it, gave people license to feel they were part of it."

There were drugs, too. Pills. And there was a danger that I would go over the edge I could have. I thank God I didn't. It was darkest during the filming of Gilbert Grape

RIGHT: The filming of *Gilbert Grape* was a dark time for Johnny, and he swore off alcohol for nine months when it had finished.

CHAPTER FIVE

What's Eating
JOHNNY DEPP?

ABOVE RIGHT: Johnny with heavy-drinking friend, Shane MacGowan, of Pogues fame.

After the split from Ryder, Johnny had his tattoo surgically altered so that instead of "Winona Forever", it read "Wino Forever" – a nod to his love of drinking and drinkers. To take control of his life, he appointed his older sister, Christie Dembrowski, now thirty-two, as his personal manager. He also started thinking about how best to invest the money he made as an actor. The first opportunity came up in early 1993, when the musician Chuck E. Weiss, a peer and friend of Tom Waits and Rickie Lee Jones, apparently called Johnny to beg him to help rescue the Central Nightclub, which was on the brink of closure. The club, which sits on the corner of Larrabee Street and Sunset Boulevard in Los Angeles, had played host to many legendary live performances. Wanting to save the venue, Johnny acquired a 51% share in the club.

According to the differing accounts of how Johnny came to have this share, some say he had already met the owner, Anthony Fox, at the club in 1992 and that the pair had discussed going into business together, the club's sudden jeopardy simply afforded an opportunity. Others tell the story of Weiss' impassioned S.O.S to Johnny. Most accounts state that he paid a reported $350,000 in return for the majority stake. After refitting the interior to give a 1920s feel, the club reopened as The Viper Room in August 1993. With a capacity for two hundred and a small dance floor area the club was intimate, designed to be a hip hangout for the lucky few in the know or invited. Shane MacGowan, solo from The Pogues, backed by

Burton had enormous problems finding studio backing, not only because the film dealt with 'someone perceived as the worst director and a transvestite' but also because he wanted to shoot in cheesy black and white in homage to Wood's films

a local Irish band hired by Johnny, inaugurated the venue with a boozy set. Within days of opening The Viper Room was *the* place to be seen in Los Angeles.

In the same month, Johnny began filming *Ed Wood*, his second outing with director Tim Burton. The film was about Edward D. Wood Jr, legendary cult director of B-movies, many of which were made with the actor Bela Lugosi. Wood, who died destitute in 1978,

ABOVE: Cult director Ed Wood (right) on the set of *Night of the Gouls* in 1959. Depp was committed to the offbeat film of his life.

having faded into obscurity, had enjoyed a period of incredible output in the 1950s, making entire films in days, most considered universally dismal. The director, though not gay, was a transvestite. What Burton had in mind was to make a film about the glory days of this colourful character focusing on the making of two Wood classics: his 1953 debut feature, *Glen or Glenda* and also 1959's *Plan 9 From Outer Space*.

Initially, Burton had enormous problems finding studio backing, not only because the film dealt with "someone perceived as the worst director and a transvestite" but also because he wanted to shoot in cheesy black and white in homage to Wood's films. Because of those twin subjects, most studios didn't want to go near the project, fearing the film would never find anything but a cult audience. Regardless, Burton called Johnny out of the blue and asked if he could meet him right away at the Formosa Café in Los Angeles. They met twenty minutes later. Over a beer Burton told Johnny about the *Ed Wood* project. From that moment Johnny, who had seen some of Wood's films, was committed to the offbeat film, even though Burton had no funding in place.

This instant commitment again speaks of the special trust and understanding between Johnny and Burton. Considering at this time Johnny had famously turned down roles in films that went on to become massive blockbusters such as Tom Cruise's part in *Interview With The Vampire*, Keanu Reeves' part in *Speed*, Woody Harrelson's part in *Indecent Proposal*, Bruce Willis' part in *Hudson Hawk* (1991), his instant commitment to *Ed Wood* makes good on the pledge he made when he left *21 Jump Street* to never again take a part for the sake of regular work, money and popularity. Much later, he would also famously turn down Leonardo DiCaprio's role in *Titanic*. Talking in 1995 of the many roles he declined, he said: "I knew *Indecent Proposal* would be a big hit, but, then, wasn't *Hudson Hawk* supposed to be big, too? I can't judge them and I don't want to try. There have been a lot of scripts I just didn't want to do." Later, he more directly said of his career choices, "I'm not a Blockbuster boy, I never wanted to be. I just don't want to look back in thirty or forty or fifty years and have my grandkids say, 'You did a lot of stupid shit, Granddad. What an idiot you were, smiling for the cameras and playing the game.'"

RIGHT: The original "glamour goul" of the 1950s, Vampira, in another of Ed Woods cult films, **Plan 9 From Outer Space**.

ABOVE: Johnny in a rare moment out of drag on the set of *Ed Wood*, with director Tim Burton and co-star Sarah Jessica Parker.

His work on *Ed Wood* was anything but "stupid shit". It earned him his third Golden Globe nomination in the Best Performance by an Actor in a Motion Picture: Comedy/Musical category. He started work on the film by reading everything he could about Wood, re-watching his films and researching the transvesticism that played such a big part in Wood's life. To do this, Johnny ordered literature from Miss Vera's Finishing School in New York, apparently a centre that advises men on the intricacies and particulars of tranvesticism. To get a feel for cross-dressing, he had a costumer source him a whole array of pumps, skirts, sweaters and slips, which he could try out and wear at home.

Meanwhile, Burton got backing for the film from Disney, and armed with a cast that included Johnny, Martin Landau, Sarah Jessica Parker and Patricia Arquette and a modest $18 million budget, shooting started in August 1993. By then Johnny had decided to base his portrayal of Ed Wood on a medley of Ronald Reagan, the Tin Man in *The Wizard of Oz* and Casey Kasem. He was also now very comfortable in drag, so much so that he even went out for a drink in character. Burton has said that it was the strength of Johnny's acting that superceded the initial passing novelty of seeing the actor in drag: "I was concerned about the fact that Ed would have to be in drag through portions of the film. People in drag are a real easy target. But Johnny is so credible that he pulls it off without making it laughable."

Filming ended in November 1993. The shoot had been very different to *What's Eating Gilbert Grape*.

ABOVE: Johnny as the maverick b-movie director Ed Wood.

RIGHT: Ed Wood was notorious for his cross dressing and Depp took this aspect of his character very seriously.

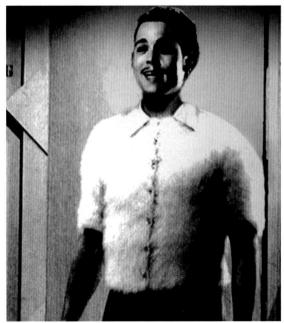

Gone was the self-medicating, the drinking. Johnny was operating with a clear head. During this time, he realized how lucky he'd been to escape the clichéd Hollywood story of addiction, or worse. In the end, he stayed sober for nine months. "I was in a bad way," he said with hindsight of the era that climaxed with him breaking up with Ryder. "It was an ugly, ugly time inside. *Ed Wood* was like a great exorcism for me. It was really a time of feeling all that pain; you know that shit I was going through. I just wanted to run. I wanted to just jump through the scene and go nuts. It was the end of something. And the beginning of something else."

ABOVE: Depp with Sarah Jessica Parker, later to shoot to fame as Carrie in *Sex and the City*, in a scene from *Ed Wood.*

RIGHT: River Phoenix, who died tragically after hanging out at The Viper Room.

This sense of having got away lightly was driven home on 30 October 1993 when fellow actor River Phoenix came to The Viper Room with his girlfriend Samantha Mathis, his brother Leaf, sister Rain and Flea, the bass guitarist in the band Red Hot Chili Peppers. Johnny knew River: the two young actors had a mutual respect for each other's work. They had occasionally talked of appearing in a project together. Shortly after midnight, River Phoenix was helped out of the club, feeling unwell. As the group and a club doorman debated what to do, Leaf made a 911 call, asking for medical assistance. By the time the paramedics arrived, it was already too late. Phoenix had died on the sidewalk outside The Viper Room. Time of death was given as 1:51 a.m. on 31 October 1993. Cause of death was given as "acute multiple drug ingestion".

The senseless death hit Johnny hard. Twice in his life, once recently, he had lived on the edge. Now he had concrete proof of what happened if you didn't wake up one morning and make some changes. In interviews he spoke of River Phoenix having made a mistake, of his shock at how the talented actor was here and then gone. As the tabloids ran with the story of Phoenix's untimely death, Johnny had to deal with media speculation that The Viper Room was permitting open drug use, an untrue rumour that hurt, especially since he had put his own wild days behind him. "All the tabloids started saying we were having drug parties," he later said. "The whole thing was weird, awful, ugly and sad. The incident is seared onto my brain, onto my heart."

CHAPTER SIX

MODEL BEHAVIOUR

ABOVE RIGHT: Supermodel Kate Moss became Johnny's next serious girlfriend after Winona Ryder.

In January 1994, Johnny met British supermodel Kate Moss, the recently appointed face of Calvin Klein, at Café Tabac in New York City. Johnny, at another table, spotted a friend sitting with a group of people including Kate. He went over, said hello to his friend and invited everyone to come over and join him at his table. Kate, who was born on 16 January 1974, had just turned twenty; Johnny was thirty. She had become a model after getting spotted at JFK airport by Sarah Doukas, founder of the Storm model agency in 1988, when she was just fourteen. By the time she met Johnny, she had risen to international notoriety, been crowned a supermodel and was best known for the nude Calvin Klein "Obsession" ads.

Although Johnny and Kate got along well, the connection wasn't instant. She later said, when asked if it was a case of love at first sight, "No, not the first moment I saw him. But I knew from the first moment we talked that we were going to be together – I've never had that before." This first meeting offered no signposts that the couple would be together for the next four years, that they would embark on a tempestuous on/off relationship that would end just before Johnny met the woman he'd been looking for his whole life.

The couple made their first public appearance together in February 1994, at the Los Angeles club, Smashbox, where Vogue magazine was throwing a benefit for the Drug Abuse Resistance Education programme (D.A.R.E). As part of the evening's events, Johnny screened an eight-and-a-half minute anti-drug film that he'd directed. Likely prompted by River Phoenix's tragic death and the tabloid hounding of Johnny and The Viper Room in the aftermath, the film's message was that drugs are no escape and there are better ways of coping, like reading and painting, with difficult situations. The making of the film harked back to the help-lines and public service announcements that ran at the end of *21 Jump Street*, which Johnny was so proud to have been involved with. Soon after, in March 1994, Johnny and Kate were seen taking a vacation together in St Bart's. Back in New York, on 5 April, they appeared at the première of John Waters' new film, *Serial Mom*. For the first time since breaking off his engagement to Winona

'Working with Marlon is the greatest thing that's happened in my life I mean.'

where do you go from here?"

LEFT: Johnny with acting idol and mentor, Marlon Brando, in *Don Juan DeMarco*.

Ryder, Depp was in a serious relationship again.

By spring 1994, Johnny was at work again on a new film called *Don Juan DeMarco* (1995). He said that the role "chose" him. When he was approached to play a troubled character who may, or may not be the world's greatest lover, by Jeremy Leven (a novelist and former psychiatrist proposing he direct a screenplay which he had adapted from his own novel for a budget of $3 million), Johnny set one condition. He would only accept the part if Marlon Brando played the part of psychiatrist Dr Jack Mickler, who tries to puncture Don Juan's delusion. Leven thought Johnny was kidding but when he realized he was serious, he said he would be more than interested in having Brando in his film. So Johnny set about making it happen: he called Brando. Although he was nervous of speaking with his favourite actor, Brando put him at ease and suggested he come over for dinner. The legend and fan shared Chinese takeout. Johnny found Brando to be a dazzling intellect and by the end of the evening, he had persuaded him to take the role.

Johnny then had to prepare for his role. Usually he did this by seeking out a personal connection with the character. For instance, with "Ed Wood", he decided that the director's transvesticism was a way of intensifying his love for women, a way to get closer to them. That helped him bring Wood alive. Now he was faced with a character claiming to be the world's most celebrated lover. While he'd had various high profile relationships, they were all long, serious and monogamous. Johnny saw himself as no Don Juan and as a consequence he had to extensively research the legend of Don Juan to find a way into the role.

Meanwhile, thanks to Johnny bringing Brando to the project, Leven's tiny film (originally penned in a Connecticut barn) became a different picture altogether. "My little $3 million movie suddenly cost $20 million," Leven said. "And I ended up directing Marlon Brando and Faye Dunaway in my first movie. Actually the costs were kept down when Brando said he would do it. Every actor in Hollywood suddenly wanted to be in it and at a fraction of their usual price; they just wanted to work with Brando."

On set Brando and the young actor had great chemistry. Faye Dunaway, who played Brando's wife in the film, said of the Brando-Depp relationship: "Brando *adores* him. He loves Johnny's genuineness and modesty and that he is who he is. You're not a great actor like Brando for nothing, you know. He knows how to recognize a sham in any shape." Johnny was blown away by the experience: "Working with Marlon is the greatest thing that's happened in my life. I mean, where do you go from here? Who would have thought? Marlon is not a myth; he's everything people think he is. He's not old, either. I can't think of him as a seventy-year-old man – he's like a seventy-year-old child, a child genius." Leven kept a close eye on the magical rapport between Johnny and Brando. "I watched Marlon help Johnny with scenes. Johnny had a scene in which his eyes partially fill with tears, but not fully. Marlon said, 'That kid is great.'"

Off set, Johnny was feeling hounded by the tabloids again. The media were chasing him and Kate Moss everywhere, wanting a piece of the celebrity couple's private life. As with Ryder, Johnny soon became impatient with the intrusion on his privacy. After the sober nine-month period that surrounded the making of *Ed Wood* he was off the wagon and drinking again. As the stress mounted, two events happened. The first involved a sudden health scare. "I was living on coffee and cigarettes," Depp later explained. "No food, no sleep. I was sitting around with some pals when my heart started running at two hundred beats a minute." He was rushed to hospital. "I got a shot, boom! A shot that basically stops your heart for a second. Now there's an experience that'll scare you into shape."

The second event happened in September 1994, while Johnny was staying at the Mark Hotel in New York doing interviews for *Ed Wood*. On 12 September Kate Moss checked in to join him. At 5 a.m. on 13 September the hotel desk received reports of a fracas that was taking place in Room 1410. The complaint came from a guest in an adjoining room. The guest was Roger Daltrey, singer with The Who. He called down to reception and said there was a lot of banging

ABOVE: The relationship between Kate Moss and Johnny Depp was great fodder for the press and they were hounded everywhere.

RIGHT: Out on the town.

and crashing going on in the room next door. The hotel sent up a security guard to see what was going on. Apparently, the guard summoned Johnny to the door and after surveying for damage (presumably broken furniture and furnishings) demanded the star immediately check out. Johnny, after explaining

'I got a shot, boom! A shot that basically stops your heart for a second. Now there's an experience that'll scare you into shape'

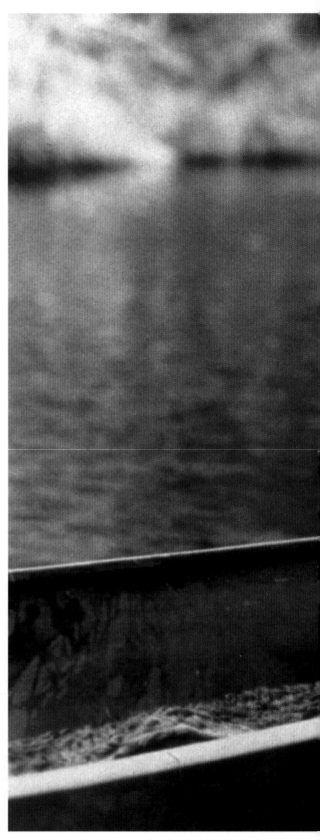

ABOVE and RIGHT: Johnny in Jim Jarmusch's philosophical Western, *Dead Man,* **a role that killed off Johnny's teen pin-up image once and for all.**

that he would pay for any damage he had caused to the room, politely refused to leave the suite. The guard called the police, who subsequently arrested him. He was escorted from the hotel in handcuffs, taken to Precinct House and held in jail. The police explained that he had been arrested on two counts of "criminal mischief". Presenting a list of damages, the hotel requested $9767.12. Dismissed by a judge, Johnny was ordered to pay the charges.

In 2004 Depp said of that night's events: "Very simply, I had a bad day. I'd been chased by paparazzi and was feeling a little bit like novelty boy." Of trashing the room, he told *Playboy*: "I lost it. It was the culmination of many things, a bad spark, and I went off. I did what I felt was necessary. Thank God it wasn't a human being but a hotel room that I took it out on! It was a weird incident. There was a hotel security guard, who was really kind of pissy and arrogant – I wanted to pop him. But I knew that if I did it would obviously be a horse of a different color: lawsuits and

What amazed me about Johnny was his ability to go through a lot of very subtle but big changes ever telegraphing that character development.

God knows what else. I did my business and they came up to the room. By that point I had cooled down. I said, 'I'll of course pay for any damages, I apologize.' That wasn't enough. The guy got snooty and shitty. The next thing you know, the police were at the door."

Killing off rumours that the incident in the hotel

room put an end to their relationship, Johnny and Kate appeared together on 24 September 1994 at the première of *Ed Wood*. The next day they were out again, attending a Paediatric AIDS Foundation carnival. Later the same evening, Johnny threw a party at the Metronome club on Broadway in honour

Me Drinking". Johnny, who had known MacGowan for some time, had also directed and starred in the promo video for the single. This wasn't his only musical outing at the time. He had also been moonlighting in an occasional fun band called P (or Pee) with Gibby Hayes from Texan band The Butthole Surfers, Flea from Red Hot Chili Peppers and Steve Jones, former guitarist with The Sex Pistols.

Johnny had meanwhile committed to a Western called *Dead Man*, for which director Jim Jarmusch was trying to get financing. He was lined up to play William Blake, an accountant who heads out to the unexplored West at the end of the nineteenth century. Finding the job for which he had arrived taken by another applicant, he ends up in a chain of events that leave him unjustly on the run as an outlaw with little time left to live. Philosophical, thin on plot, shot in elegant black and white, it was the anti-commercial vehicle Johnny had been praying would come along.

It also gave him a chance to work with Jarmusch, a key American independent filmmaker he already counted as a friend. Possessing a European cinematic sensibility, Jarmusch, who directed Winona Ryder in *Night On Earth* (1991), was known for his defiant, uncompromising attitude to making films and dealing with producers. The pairing of Jarmusch and Johnny, both rebel spirits, came about after Jarmusch wrote the part of William Blake especially for Johnny. "I wrote this film with Johnny Depp in my head for the character of Blake," he said. "I knew Johnny and told him the story before I even wrote it. If he had refused or not been interested, I'm not sure I would have made the film."

Studios raised similar concerns to those that met Tim Burton when he was trying to get *Ed Wood* off the ground. They weren't happy about Jarmusch's intention to shoot in black and white, nor with his screenplay that debunked the clichés of formula genre Westerns. Once again, Johnny committed to the project long before Jarmusch found a studio willing to back the film. Asked if she minded her client taking the path of most resistance all the time, Johnny's

in his character, out of sequence but without

of Mickey Rourke's birthday. The message was loud and clear: he and Kate were anything but over.

In October 1994, Johnny strapped on a guitar and made an entertaining guest appearance with Shane MacGowan on the British TV show *Top of The Pops*, performing MacGowan's single "This Woman's Got

agent Tracey Jacobs said, "He had an allegiance to Tim Burton and stuck with that process for almost six months. He did the exact same thing for *Dead Man*." And how did she feel about her client passing on blockbusters like *Speed*? "Am I disappointed that he turned those projects down? No. Do I want him to be in a movie that does $400 million? Of course, *I'm not stupid!* Let me make this really clear to you: he wants to be in a commercial movie. It just has to be the right timing and the right one, that's all! Hopefully he'll be available when those come along again."

Eventually, Johnny's involvement earned Jarmusch a $9 million budget and filming began. Jarmusch was delighted with the route the actor took. "What I love about Johnny for this character," he said. "Is that he has the ability to start off very innocently. This is a difficult role to play, to start off as a passive character in a genre that is based on active, aggressive central characters. What amazed me about Johnny was his ability to go through a lot of very subtle but big changes in his character, out of sequence but without ever telegraphing that character development. He was much

BELOW: The perfect couple, Kate adjusts Johnny's bow tie at the Cannes Film Festival.

RIGHT: Johnny playing against type in the slick thriller *Nick of Time*. Many assumed he took this part in search of commercial kudos.

more precise than I thought he would be. He was also very inventive." Of Johnny Depp the person he noted: "He's moody and very emotional and very sensitive. In real life, sometimes, it's hard for him to decide where to eat or what to do, but as an actor he's very precise." The film, which had been shot on location in Sedona, Arizona and Virginia City, wrapped at the end of 1994. Johnny and Kate spent Christmas in Aspen, Colorado. They rented a house and tried their hand at skiing. "I was alright actually," said Moss of the vacation. "I got on these skis and I was, like, a natural. I was good, I was. It was really funny. Yeah, I had a laugh."

On 16 January 1995 Kate Moss turned twenty-one. To celebrate, Johnny threw a surprise party for her at The Viper Room. "They opened the curtains and there was my mum, my dad and everyone had flown in from London and New York," she recalled. "And John Galliano had come from Paris. It was amazing. I was like, shaking. You know when you start to dance and your legs don't work? I had to go into the office for ten minutes till I'd calmed down." Johnny had also arranged for Thelma Houston and Gloria Gaynor to sing "Happy Birthday" to her. "Gloria Gaynor said, 'Happy birthday Miss Moss.' I was like, 'Oh my God!'"

Next, Johnny took a part in *Nick of Time* (1995, that filmed April to June 1995. In the big budget thriller, directed by John Badham, he played Gene Watson, a Los Angeles accountant suddenly faced with an impossible dilemma. Watson is escorting his daughter home from his ex-wife's funeral when kidnappers snatch her. He's then given a photograph of an individual and a gun and told that if he doesn't kill this person within the next hour and fifteen minutes, then his daughter will be murdered. Although the role gave Johnny the opportunity to act opposite Christopher Walken, the film was so different to the majority of his prior roles that many assumed he was seeking out a box-office smash. Johnny insisted otherwise, saying he took the part because he wanted to work with Badham

RIGHT: Depp in a scene from the big budget thriller *Nick of Time*, which gave him the opportunity to act opposite Christopher Walken.

FAR RIGHT: Johnny with Kate Moss. Benicio Del Toro is to his left.

and Walken, whose previous work he had admired. Regardless, watching the film, he doesn't seem engaged or connected compared to his incredible performances in *Dead Man*, *Ed Wood*, *What's Eating Gilbert Grape* and *Edward Scissorhands*. Such is his affection for outsiders or "freaks" as he has called some of the characters he's played, that in playing a straight role like that of "Gene Watson", his performance rings hollow.

Johnny and Kate then spent time together in France, a holiday tied around appearing at the Cannes Film Festival, where *Dead Man* and *Don Juan DeMarco* were both screening. Then Johnny flew to Ireland to begin work on his next film, *Divine Rapture*, which would reunite him with Marlon Brando. Johnny got involved after Brando sent him the script, saying he had committed to the project and he thought Johnny should too and join him in Ireland. Brando, seventy-one, was set to play a priest alongside Debra Winger, John Hurt and Johnny, who had the role of a journalist investigating reports of miracles in a small town. The scheduled eight-week shoot came to an abrupt end when financing was pulled just two weeks into filming. Of this abrupt end, Johnny said: "It was like being in the middle of good sex and then having the lights turn on and fifteen people with machine guns come in and say, 'Stop or die.'"

Once more Johnny left for France and took another short holiday with Kate because his next project, *The Cull*, written and slated to be directed by cult figure Donald Cammell, was set to start filming in London in September 1995. Johnny figured he'd stay in Europe for the rest of the summer, then cross the Channel. However, the film, put together by the same producers as *Divine Rapture*, suffered the same financial fate and the project collapsed. On hearing the news he returned to Los Angeles and began what would become a six-month sabbatical from acting.

But the break from work cleared his head. During the sabbatical he also began to see the humorous side of being a pin-up and movie star. Despite his every effort to shake off the *21 Jump Street* heart-throb tag, he still

LEFT: Once known as "The Castle", the house cost Johnny a reported $2.3 million.

ABOVE: Showing signs of settling down, Johnny bought Bela Lugosi's old house in Los Angeles.

received masses of mail, much of it from fans pledging undying love or lust. "I get nude pictures in the mail, yes – tons of them. Some are beautiful, nicely lit, black-and-white, mysterious. Some are out-and-out primitive. Then there are the pubes. I've gotten a lot of pubic hairs in the mail. I don't save them. I guess you could get ritualistic about it, burn the pubes in a fire, but I'm not sure I want to touch them so I throw them away."

Johnny wasn't sitting at home with his feet up, though. He used the break to move towards his dream of directing. Upon receiving a screenplay adaptation of Gregory MacDonald's novel, *The Brave* (1997), he acquired the rights and, with his brother Danny, set about revising the script into a film he could direct. The brothers worked on the screenplay at Johnny's rented home in Laurel Canyon. After years of living out of a suitcase, he was also thinking of buying his first home. In October 1995, en hommage to *Ed Wood* (in which Martin Landau had played Bela Lugosi), he purchased Lugosi's old house. The mansion, once known as "The Castle" sits off Sunset. The plot, 2.5 acres in size, is walled and gated. He acquired it for a reported $2.3 million. Finally, at the age of thirty-two, he was setting down roots.

At this time various tabloids ran reports speculating that Johnny's relationship with Kate Moss was on the wane, that having bought a house, he was now thinking

ABOVE: Spread over 2.5 acres, the walled and gated property sits just off Sunset Boulevard.

of starting a family, while the much younger Moss had no intention of taking on such responsibility. Other reports speculated that the couple were busy discussing wedding plans. In response, that October, Kate said, "He's just my boyfriend: that's all. We're not getting married." Soon after, Johnny quashed the rumours too, saying, "It's fiction. I can guarantee you that if I woke up one day with a wild hair up my ass to get hitched, there wouldn't be invitations. We'd run out and do it." He also said, "I love Kate more than anything, certainly enough to marry her. But as far as putting our names on paper, making weird public vows that signify ownership, it's not on the cards." That Christmas the couple again passed the holiday season in Aspen, their happy presence around town a rebuff to the tabloid stories.

CHAPTER SEVEN

FEAR AND LOATHING

ABOVE RIGHT: Johnny in terrific mafia film, *Donnie Brasco.*

In January 1995 Johnny threw a big party at a London restaurant for Kate Moss's twenty-second birthday. This was also when the couple are famously rumoured to have stayed at the Portobello Hotel on Stanley Gardens in Notting Hill and requested, as per celebrity myth, that the free-standing bath tub in Room 16 be filled with champagne. They then went out for dinner, leaving the tub full. To their horror when they returned, it was empty. A maid had apparently entered the room, clocked the tub filled with what she assumed to be old bath water and, quite logically, pulled the plug.

In February 1996 Johnny went to work on *Donnie Brasco* (1997), a film which saw him cast alongside another screen legend, Al Pacino. The film told the story of FBI agent Joe Pistone, who famously infiltrated the Bonnano New York-based Mafia family in the 1970s by assuming the identity of a fictitious jewel thief called "Donnie Brasco". His undercover work led to the conviction and sentencing of 120 mobsters. Under the direction of Mike Newell, Johnny was cast as Brasco and Al Pacino as his sidekick: wise-guy mentor Benjamin "Lefty" Ruggiero. Newell said

ABOVE: Johnny with Al Pacino on the set of *Donnie Brasco*.

of casting Johnny: "This particular role interested him, I think, because the whole character had to run beneath the surface, as it were. Johnny is one of those actors, who acts in a kind of long term. You stay with his characterizations throughout a film because he tells you his story in his own good time. And more important, you are willing to wait for it."

As preparation, Johnny spent time with Pistone, discussing his story, his part, studying the former FBI agent's mannerisms, the intonation of his speech. Pistone was more than impressed with the actor's dedication, as was Mike Newell who noted:

"Johnny is, in part, a great impersonator. When he met Joe Pistone I could see him latch on to certain characteristics within seconds. Joe is a man whose exterior is stony. He's very calm, very collected and you could mistake it for gentleness, but it isn't. He is a hard man, not a gentle soul, with these dead stone impenetrable eyes. I would not want to get beaten up by Joe, truly." By the time filming wrapped in June 1995 Johnny had spent several illuminating months by Al Pacino's side. He spoke very highly of working with him. Perhaps influenced by the veteran actor Johnny turned in a considered, mature performance.

From *Donnie Brasco*, he went straight on to work on his directorial debut, *The Brave*. With a budget of $7 million and a cast headed up by Marlon Brando and Frederick Forrest, filming began in August. Because of its subject matter it had been difficult to raise financing. The story concerned a dirt-poor American Indian family. Fresh out of jail, the downtrodden man of the house, Raphael, is offered a life-changing amount of money in return for making a "snuff" movie, in which he would actually be killed on film and the result distributed on the black market. Johnny was attracted to the story because it was about a husband and father who is prepared to make the ultimate sacrifice in order to improve the lives of his wife and children. As with *Ed Wood* and *Dead Man*, producers were scared off by the risqué content. However, those who were interested told Johnny that if he also appeared in the film, they could get him a budget of $5 million. But then Johnny got Marlon Brando to agree to appear and the budget shot up to $7 million.

Once filming started, Johnny found the multi-tasking exhausting. Having been used only to the actor's role, suddenly he was responsible for everything. The pressure soon got to him. Later he said that the experience of directing himself was "awful". He found it draining to deal with money, insurance and trade-union regulations, all the aspects of making a film that he didn't usually get involved with. At the end of each day, he despised seeing himself in the rushes, something he avoids when acting. On set the only comfort was the paternal presence of Marlon Brando. "For Marlon to come in and do this part for me was one of the greatest gifts that I've ever been given in my life," Johnny later said. "He was so insightful, so helpful to me as a friend, as an actor and as a director." During the shoot he was incredibly consumed and later said that the overwhelming work-load had affected

BELOW: Johnny with Iggy Pop. The veteran rocker scored Johnny's directorial debut, *The Brave*.

'He's not like a Method actor, osmosis is what he used.' Terry Gilliam

his relationships with everybody in his life, most notably Kate Moss. At that time he was working up to eighteen hours a day, agonizing over all the details, trying to cover everything. He barely had time for sleep, let alone sustaining and nurturing relationships.

On 10 May 1997 *The Brave* premièred at the Cannes Film Festival on the insistence of one of the film's producers. Not having finished the film when he learned it had been entered in competition at Cannes, Johnny raced to complete his debut. With a score by Iggy Pop, it finally went off to competition. When the film screened, Johnny said he received a standing ovation from such esteemed directors as Bernardo Bertolucci and Emir Kusturica. He was delighted. But then, the next morning, the all-important first wave of reviews broke and the critics savaged the film. He was dismayed. The reviews killed the film's possibilities and it met the same fate as *Arizona Dream*. It was released in Europe, where it found many admirers but never in the USA.

Johnny's next project was no less personal. He signed up to play Raoul Duke in an adaptation of *Fear and Loathing in Las Vegas*, the infamous 1971

book by gonzo journalist Hunter S. Thompson, whom Johnny had admired since he was teenager. He first met the drink, drug and gun-loving writer over Christmas 1995 while holidaying in Aspen with Kate Moss, her mother and her brother Nick. One evening Johnny took the Moss clan to Thompson's local hangout, the Woody Creek Tavern, hoping to encounter the writer. Late in the evening

ABOVE: Johnny in Terry Gilliam's adaptation of Hunter S. Thompson's *Fear and Loathing in Las Vegas*.

Thompson entered the bar in typically charismatic fashion, wielding a pair of crackling cattle prods.

Johnny introduced himself to Thompson, who knew little of the actor beyond having seen a few scenes from *Cry-Baby*, and they had drinks. He found the writer hilarious. As the evening grew late, Thompson invited them back to his nearby ranch. Impressed by a weapon in Thompson's gun collection, Johnny was treated to a Thompson spectacular at two in the morning. Thompson handed him a propane tank and a small matchbox-sized cache of nitroglycerin that he asked him to tape to the propane tank. They then went out to the backyard, where Johnny was instructed to shoot the antique weapon he'd been so impressed by at the explosive device. He did so, and a 75-foot explosion ripped up the Colorado sky. But Kate Moss's mother was unimpressed: she thought Thompson was insane. Sensing this, Thompson went out of his way to assure Moss's mother that the stunt was perfectly safe and nothing more than a bit of fun. Looking back on the evening, Moss later said: "The whole evening, I will never forget it – it was just so mad. My mum being there, the bomb."

With Terry Gilliam directing and upcoming actor Benicio Del Toro cast as Duke's sidekick, Dr Gonzo, Johnny threw himself into intensive research for the part. He moved into Thompson's house and set up camp in the basement, where he slept on a sofa bed beside a keg of gunpowder. By day, he studied Thompson's old notebooks – the ones that inspired and shaped *Fear and Loathing in Las Vegas*. He read sections from the book out loud to Thompson, who would patiently correct his delivery, and around the clock, he studied the writer's mannerisms and quirks.

Johnny left Colorado and drove back to Los Angeles in Thompson's "Red Shark" Chevy convertible wearing some of the clothes the writer was wearing in 1971 and had kept in storage. When he met Terry Gilliam in LA at the end of the trip, Gilliam was astonished by the transformation, noting, "He's not like a Method actor – osmosis is what he used." The next time Johnny went to see Thompson in Colorado, he arrived with the centre of his head shaved to mimic Thompson's appearance. But Thompson didn't feel it was accurate enough, so he sat Johnny down and proceeded to shave his head that little bit further until the likeness was uncanny.

The shoot started in July 1997 and lasted eleven weeks. By the end of filming Johnny felt he had spent so much time with, or playing Thompson that he had trouble breaking out of character. To create a segue from set to home, he left the shoot with a souvenir prop: an eight-foot yellow gorilla with "You Can Run But You Cannot Hide" emblazoned across its stomach. Johnny installed the gorilla in his front yard, a none-too subtle message to his neighbours.

"I thought, 'Aah, I've got a good idea,'" he said of the prank. "I'll rig him up for those bastard neighbours who've been complaining about the construction and fucking leaves in their garden. That was horrible shit. They're real trainspotters, real nit-pickers. I had the construction crew on the film build his hand so he was flicking the bird. He also has a giant erection. We built a pump into him so he's constantly peeing into a bucket. The neighbours haven't commented on him yet, but they must know he was put there especially for them. I've had him moved now, but he used to stand facing their little veranda where they sit and have coffee every morning."

Always with one eye on music, Johnny's latest bit of guitar playing was released in August 1997. He had contributed slide guitar to the track "Fade In-Out" on the new Oasis album, *Be Here Now*. Apparently Noel Gallagher was too drunk to record the slide part and Johnny, a friend of the Gallagher brothers, happened to be in the studio in Mustique with the band at the time. He stepped into Noel's shoes and nailed the part in one take. Gallagher said on the eve of the album's release, "It's going to be weird how that's perceived, having a Hollywood star on the album. But I'm glad it happened. If he hadn't been around, we'd have had to get some fat old geezer who'd be telling us about how he played with Clapton in '76 and did a slide solo that lasted for fucking months!"

In January 1998 Johnny went to work on *The Astronaut's Wife* (1999), written and directed by Rand Ravich. The shoot would last until spring. He played Commander Spencer Armacost, a superficially wholesome character, who, on a NASA mission, loses contact with earth for 120 seconds. Back in the USA, he and his partner on the mission find themselves changed. Johnny liked the idea of playing a man who seems all-American on the outside, but on the inside is "just a full-on scumbag." Throughout the film, as with *Private Resort* or *Nick of Time*, he seems to be punching in to a job he isn't enjoying. There's a lack of presence to his performance; he looks bored. Again,

But Thompson didn't feel it was accurate enough, so he sat Johnny down and proceeded to shave his head that little bit further until the likeness was uncanny.

it confirms that if he can't find a way into a character or doesn't feel a personal connection, then the magic fails to turn up. At the box office the film's reception was poor. Despite having a $34 million budget, it only grossed $10 million when it opened in 1999 and, like *Nick of Time*, failed to find a broad audience.

Meanwhile, Johnny's relationship with Kate Moss was in its dying throes. After apparently moving into her New York apartment in early 1997, the tabloids reported that the couple's on-off relationship was off again by June 1997. Through official channels, Johnny denied that he and Moss had broken up. Regardless, tabloid stories kept appearing that alleged the couple had split, Moss apparently having had enough of fighting. In January 1998, just before Johnny started work on *The Astronaut's Wife*, he once more organized a surprise party for Moss's birthday. This time, he took her to see The Rolling Stones play at Madison Square Gardens. After

ABOVE: Depp and Benicio del Toro in *Fear and Loathing in Las Vegas*.

the show, they went to a private party at Ronnie Wood's hotel suite that lasted deep into the night.

Soon after reports circulated that Moss and Johnny had bought an apartment together on Place Dauphine in Paris. Neither ever confirmed whether this was true. But regardless, their relationship was about to come to an end anyway. In May 1998 the couple made their last public appearance together at the Cannes Film Festival, for a screening of *Fear and Loathing in Las Vegas*. Days later they announced they had broken up. Johnny said, "Kate is somebody I care about deeply. We were together for four years and she's a great, lovely, sweet, pure girl. Really a great kid and I care about her. I love her on a very deep, profound level." He put their break-up down to the complexities of carrying on a long distance relationship: "Distance is very difficult when you're trying to maintain a relationship, when you're

ABOVE: Johnny and Kate Moss at the Cannes Film Festival 1997.

He knew though that Kate Moss wasn't that woman: "We ended up living apart and only talking on the phone every two weeks. I really feel like I blew it with Kate. There's a big part of me that really misses her and I keep wondering why we aren't together, thinking about starting a family. I have a really traditional view of marriage. I want a family and a house in the country with a couple of dogs and a goldfish." All of this and more were just around the corner…

BELOW: Johnny in *The Astronaut's Wife,* one of his lesser-known roles.

thousands of miles apart for a lot of time. We still see each other, hang out and talk on the phone. We're close, but I'm not with anybody at all." He also blamed himself, saying, "I was a horrific pain in the butt to live with. I can be a total moron at times. I let my work get in the way, which made me difficult to get along with."

It would seem that his relationship with Moss came to an end for the same reasons as his previous relationships with Sherilyn Fenn, Jennifer Grey and Winona Ryder. Hectic combined work schedules, continuous media harassment and the problematic nature of a long distance relationship appeared to have once more felled a Johnny Depp relationship. And as always, on top of this, Johnny was looking for a woman to settle down with. "I want to have children," he said. "I'd really like to become a parent now but finding the right woman to share that with is proving difficult."

CHAPTER EIGHT

PARADIS FOREVER

ABOVE RIGHT: When Johnny met French singer, actress and model, Vanessa Paradis, his whole life changed.

After finishing *The Astronaut's Wife* in April and breaking up with Kate Moss in May 1998, Johnny left the USA for France to play Dean Corso in Roman Polanski's new film, *The Ninth Gate* (1999). Shot in France between June and September 1998, the role gave him a chance to clear his head, spend time away from the States and work with a director he greatly admired. Early on, when Polanski was adapting Arturo Perez-Reverte's novel *The Dumas Club* and as Jim Jarmusch did with *Dead Man*, he wrote the part of bibliophile Dean Corso with Johnny in mind.

Being in Paris for the shoot helped Johnny clear his head after the break up with Moss. The short stay away from the USA was to have lasting effects on his life, though. As he later said with hindsight, "I came over here to make a movie, met a girl, got a place, had a baby." The girl was French singer, actress and model Vanessa Paradis. Born in Paris on 22 December 1972, she found international fame with the hit single "Joe Le Taxi" when she was just fourteen. Aside from a successful singing career, which has included a collaboration with French legend Serge Gainsbourg, Paradis has also appeared in various films like *Noce blanche* (1989) and *La Fille sur le Pont* (1999) and modelled, most notably as the face of Chanel's Coco perfume.

While filming *The Ninth Gate*, Johnny, who had met

LEFT: Vanessa Paradis in the 1999 film, *La Fille sur le Pont*.

ABOVE: Johnny in Roman Polanski's supernatural thriller, *The Ninth Gate*.

Paradis before, spotted her crossing the lobby of the Hotel Costes in Paris. "We met briefly years ago," he recalled. "I remember thinking, 'Ouch!' It was just hello, but the contact was electric. That was in 1993. It wasn't until 1998, when I went to do the Polanski film *The Ninth Gate* and was in the lobby of the hotel getting messages. I turned around and across the lobby saw this back. She had on a dress with an exposed back. I thought, 'Wow!' Suddenly the back turned and she looked at me. I walked right over, and there were those eyes again – I knew it was her. She asked, 'Do you remember me?' I said, 'Oh yeah.' We had a drink, and it was over with at that point – I knew I was in big trouble."

The split from Moss, though, was still very fresh in his mind: the last thing he was looking for was another relationship. But he later admitted that when he saw Paradis in the hotel lobby, it was love at first sight. "I pretty much fell in love with Vanessa the moment I set eyes on her," he said. "As a person I was pretty much a lost cause at that point

'He used to hide fart machines in people's costumes and operate them by remote control.'

LEFT: *The Ninth Gate* gave Johnny a chance to work in Paris with a director he admired.

ABOVE: *Sleepy Hollow* saw Johnny team up yet again with Tim Burton.

of my life. She turned all that around for me with her incredible tenderness and understanding. She made me feel like a real human being instead of someone Hollywood had manufactured. It sounds incredibly corny and phoney, but that's exactly what happened to me and what she has meant to me."

The couple started dating and were instantly a new target for the media. Roman Polanski commented that Johnny would often arrive exhausted on set because the photographers and reporters were incessantly hounding him. That summer, Johnny and Vanessa were inseparable. By the time The *Ninth Gate* shoot had wrapped in September 1998 she was pregnant. It seemed that Johnny had finally found the woman he had been looking for, a woman who also wanted to start a family, settle down.

Meanwhile, things were going less well for Kate Moss. In November 1998 she checked herself into the Priory Clinic to receive treatment for exhaustion. In a brief statement, she said, "I've been doing a lot of work

and too much partying." When the media learned that one of the world's biggest supermodels was in a rehab clinic, they jumped on the story. Rumours were abundant. Some theorized that the break-up with Depp, his new found happiness and impending parenthood with Paradis, were behind the model's personal crisis. Others ran with an untrue story that Johnny had sent Moss a BMW as a get-well present. Just before Christmas 1998 she left The Priory and went back to work in January 1999, doing the first shows she said she had done sober in ten years. She revealed this in a candid interview with *The Face*, published in March 1999, explaining that her treatment at The Priory had been for drinking. Saying that her "chosen tipple" was "Anything. Given the choice, vodka," she went on to add: "I was in denial for a long time, I think. I could have carried on drinking but I was beginning to not be very happy. It stops working after a while. A bit messy." When asked what prompted her decision to check into The Priory, she said: "I couldn't keep

Hollow (1999), a film in which he would play "Ichabod Crane". Based on Washington Irving's story 'The Legend of Sleepy Hollow", the film was set in a small upstate New York town in 1799. Crane, a bumbling constable, is posted to the town to investigate a series of grisly murders supposedly committed by the local legend: a headless horseman. During the case he meets the love of his life, Katrina Van Tassel, played by Christina Ricci. The film was shot in the UK between November 1998 and April 1999, principally at Leavesden Studios. Before shooting began, Johnny decided to base his interpretation of Crane on Angela Lansbury's performance in *Death on the Nile* (1978).

On set, the larking about that Johnny had perfected to pass time on the set of *21 Jump Street* was again present in abundance. Co-star Michael Gambon said of these pranks, "He used to hide fart machines in people's costumes and operate them by remote control. He had a special rubber one that Marlon Brando gave him. I thought I was good at it, but he's the real professional."

During the shoot, on the evening of Saturday, 30 January 1999, the incessant hounding from the media again took Johnny to breaking point. He and a pregnant Paradis went for dinner at Marco Pierre White's Mirabelle restaurant in London. The dinner became notorious because the bill came to a reported £17,000, including £11,000 for a single bottle of Romanée Conti 1978 Burgundy; also, for what happened when the couple left the restaurant. Encountering paparazzi, Johnny told them that he did not want them taking pictures of Paradis pregnant. "I just decided, look, this is my girl. This is our first baby. I'm not going to let you fucking people turn this into a circus. You ain't turning this deeply, profoundly beautiful, spiritual, life-changing experience into a novelty. Not without a fight!"

The photographers were insistent they were going to take pictures so Johnny told Paradis to get in the car so they couldn't take photographs of her belly. Then, he got in the car with her. He was unable to close the door, though, because one of the paparazzi was

myself in check any more. Couldn't do it. I kind of lost the plot really there a little bit." Moss also refuted the story that Depp had sent her a BMW. Instead, she explained, Rover had sent her a Mini Cooper. "Suddenly it turned into a BMW that Johnny gave me. How did a Mini Cooper suddenly transform into a BMW from Johnny Depp? Where did that come from?" She did, however, admit that Johnny had been "very supportive" of her decision to seek treatment. Also, when asked how many times in her life she had been in love, she said that only once, with Johnny, "I was in love with him and I haven't been in love with anyone since. It was quite an intense relationship for four years and for a while there it seemed kind of like it wasn't real. But it was." On why they broke-up, she said there were "a lot of reasons, I think. Both of us."

In November 1998 Johnny went to work with Tim Burton for a third time, this time on *Sleepy*

keeping it open. "He had his hand wedged in there," Johnny later said of the evening. "I looked down at the ground and there was a 17-inch wooden plank, a two-by-two or something. Instinct took over. I picked it up and whacked the guy's hand. I went outside and said, 'Now I want you to take my picture because the first fucking guy who hits a flash, I'm going to kick his skull in! Let's go, take my picture!' They didn't take my picture. I was livid. They walked backward down the street. I walked them away from Vanessa in the car and down this other street. It was beautiful; it was well worth it. It was kind of poetic. The next thing I knew, I saw flashing lights on the buildings around me."

A police car arrived. It was almost midnight.

BELOW: Johnny as Lieutenant Victor in Julien Schnabel's *Before Night Falls.*

Johnny was arrested and taken to a West London police station, where he was held for questioning for four hours and then released with a caution at approximately 5:20 a.m. Again, as with the incident at the hotel in Vancouver and at the Mark Hotel, no charges were pressed. Once more, the media hounding had proved too much for him.

On 6 March 1999 Johnny received an Honorary César at the French Césars for his work to date. Several days later, on 12 March 1999 a special charity episode of British TV show *The Vicar of Dibley* aired on Red Nose Day in aid of Comic Relief. In the episode, Johnny appeared as himself. Supposedly shooting his latest film in Dibley, Geraldine (Dawn French) invites him over to the vicarage for a party with his Hollywood friends. But then there's a power cut in the village so she never gets to see who is in his famous entourage.

When *Sleepy Hollow* wrapped, Johnny decided to take a break. He had been working non-stop since *Donnie Brasco*. He finished work in April 1999 and wouldn't work again until September. The decision was of course influenced by the arrival of his daughter, Lily-Rose Melody Depp, who was born on 27 May 1999 at 8:25 p.m. Johnny has spoken of the birth as a personal epiphany: "As of May 27, 1999, at 8.25 p.m, suddenly everything became clear. I felt like for thirty-six years, I'd walked around in a fog, not really living." And also: "I went through thirty-five years of a very strange and dark fog. I never really understood what the point was to anything in life. I knew that I had some degree of luck and success in my chosen field, in my business and work. I knew that I was very lucky and my family, my mom, my sisters and my brother, my dad is okay. I had good friends and stuff like that. It wasn't until Vanessa and then the birth of our daughter, Lily-Rose that I finally realized that there is something to live for. I then knew why I had to be alive. There was a reason to live."

From Johnny's comments, it's clear that becoming a parent changed him overnight. The arrival of his daughter completed the picture. Now he had his dream woman and dream child, his life-long traditional hopes had materialized, an anchor had dropped, life was different… he had a family now. But now the couple had a child the media hounding was worse than before with photographers desperately seeking shots of either Lily-Rose or the family. Of the hounding, Johnny singled out *Voici* magazine for his frustrations. "I had an incident with a really dumb magazine called *Voici*," he told *Esquire*. "Where they printed a photograph of Lily Rose, a long-lens shot from very far away and I just went ballistic. You can sue them. I've sued a couple of times, Vanessa's sued and we win every time but this time I was beyond suing. I just wanted to beat whoever was responsible into the earth. I just wanted to rip him apart. They can do anything they want to me. And most tabloids have. But not my kid: not my pure, innocent little baby – she didn't ask to be in this circus."

Johnny went back to work in September 1999

RIGHT: Johnny also played Bon Bon, a tranvestite, in *Before Night Falls*.

playing not one but two small roles (both for no fee) in *Before Night Falls* (2000), the second film by artist Julian Schnabel. In the first role he played "Lieutenant Victor", a macho Latin military man. In the other, "Bon Bon", a transvestite. The film was based on the memoirs of Cuban writer Reinaldo Arenas. Schnabel, who already knew Johnny and had asked

him personally if he wanted to appear in the film, revealed in an interview that Johnny had seen his debut film, *Basquiat* (1996), a biopic of Schnabel's peer and fellow painter, a total of fourteen times. The cameo was a sign that Johnny's priorities had changed since becoming a parent. Now that he had a family and a real sense of home, the last thing he wanted to do was undertake a protracted work schedule. He wanted to nest with his partner and daughter, revel in the elusive perfect family life he'd always craved.

But another small part that lured Johnny into interrupting his new family life was Sally Potter's *The Man Who Cried* (2000). Shot in France and England, Johnny was able to bring his wife and daughter

with him. Now mostly based in France, he enjoyed the distance from Hollywood and its competitive, claustrophobic landscape. "All I want is for the opportunity to do my work as best I can and hang around with my family, drink wine and smoke cigarettes," he told a reporter on set. "That's all it's about for me." Filming lasted from September to November 1999, with Johnny playing the part of "Cesar", a horse-riding gypsy. Highlighting the plight of Jews and gypsies in Nazi-occupied Paris, the film gave him the chance to work with Sally Potter, whose earlier film, *Orlando* (1992), he rated very highly. For the part of "Cesar", which teamed him once more with Christina Ricci, he had two gold teeth fitted. The role was once more a typical Johnny Depp character: an outcast, an alien, put upon by society. Johnny knew the emotional terrain all too well and delivered a terrific performance.

When released in 2000, however, the film was not, however, a box-office success. Nor was *Before Night Falls*, which though faring better, was mostly admired within the art-house crowd. Even Johnny by this point appeared to be resigned to his lack of commercial appeal. It was just a given that he primarily picked offbeat roles in films that, with few exceptions, rarely did well at the box office.

This run of commercial flops soon came to an end, though. When *Sleepy Hollow* opened at the end of 1999, it became a massive hit in the USA, taking $31 million over the opening weekend. After the

BELOW: Johnny Depp with Christina Ricci in *The Man Who Cried*. Playing an outcast, his role in this film was more typical of Depp.

ABOVE: Depp in *The Man Who Cried*.

success of *Edward Scissorhands* and the commercial
flop of *Ed Wood*, the Depp-Burton partnership was
seemingly back on form. The success of *Sleepy Hollow*
was no doubt helped by the uncharacteristic amount
of publicity that Johnny agreed to do for the film.

After pushing *Sleepy Hollow* so hard, Johnny and
Vanessa Paradis entered 2000 dividing their time
between their apartment in Montmartre, Paris;
the former Bela Lugosi house in Los Angeles and
a new rural farmhouse they'd bought just outside

of St Tropez in the South of France. Johnny loved this
new rural idyllic life. "It's wonderful to be living in a
tiny village with nothing around," he enthused. "There
is still the possibility to live a simple life. You can go
to the market, walk about, buy fruits and vegetables,
the things they did one hundred and two hundred
years ago." It seemed that the wild Johnny Depp
of old was finally mellowing out. About to turn
forty, no longer interested in getting drunk and
hanging out at The Viper Room, here he was
living blissfully on a farm in France with his
partner, daughter and various animals, including
a wild boar, a dog, some ponies and cats.

CHAPTER NINE

BLOW

ABOVE RIGHT: Johnny with Juliette Binoche in *Chocolat*.

In the early months of 2000 Johnny prepared to team up again with Lasse Halstrom, the director of *What's Eating Gilbert Grape*, for his new film, *Chocolat* (2000). He was signed up to play "Roux", another gypsy and outsider. Featuring a cast of strong female leads – Juliette Binoche, Lena Olin and Judi Dench – the film would go on to gross more than $70 million at the box office. In May 2000 filming began and ended in August of the same year. Once again the location was England and France, enabling Johnny to travel with his family. But this had become standard: he didn't want

to miss a second of his daughter growing up so the only solution was to take his family wherever he went.

Halstrom, who based his interpretation of "Roux" on Shane MacGowan, was thrilled to be once again working with Johnny. "I'm grateful that he agreed to do it," he said. "Despite the fact that it's a part introduced one hour into the movie. We worked together on *What's Eating Gilbert Grape* and I think he felt that he owed me to show up again. He's a great actor with great taste and classy choices." Johnny said he took the part so he could work again with Lasse Halstrom

but also with Juliette Binoche, whose performance in *Les Amants du Pont-Neuf* (1991) he had loved. Although apparently "not a huge fan of chocolate", regardless of this he enjoyed the shoot enormously. He spoke of "Roux" as a happy outcast, a man totally at ease with his status as an outsider. Was this how Johnny felt at the time? Like he was happy being on the outside? Living in France? Continuing to take the risky roles no other leading male actor would chance?

From *Chocolat*, Johnny went to work on his first lead since *Sleepy Hollow*, playing George Jung in Ted Demme's *Blow* (2001). Ted, the nephew of director Jonathan Demme (of 1993's *Philadelphia* fame) had long admired Johnny's work. And Johnny had admired Ted's debut, *Beautiful Girls* (1996), starring Matt Dillion and the young Natalie Portman. Based on a true story, *Blow* was about a small-town American, George Jung, who went from neighbourhood drug dealing to brokering deals with Colombian drug cartels, which, as a result, flooded the USA with cocaine. In the process he made between $300–$600 million but today he is serving a jail sentence that is not due to end until 2015.

As research, Johnny twice visited Jung in the Otisville Federal Correctional Institute in New York state. Incarcerated until 2015, Jung was introduced to Johnny by Ted Demme. Held over two days, the meetings were complicated to arrange and Johnny had to work fast to gain all the insight he needed. Just as he did for *Fear and Loathing in Las Vegas*, Johnny spent those two days mastering every detail of Jung's persona: how he spoke, how he walked, his mannerisms, tics. Demme was surprised at how much Johnny and Jung had in common: "I was amazed by the amount of philosophical things they agree upon. They both worship Bob Dylan and love Jack Kerouac. It was fun watching them mould into one."

Johnny liked Jung enormously, as always, picking out characteristics in his character he could relate to. In several interviews he said that had he not developed his rock'n'roll dreams when he was twelve and subsequently found a purpose and drive, he could have ended up going down the same path as Jung. This was

the personal connection that allowed him to enter the character completely. He played George as an emblem of what could have been in his own life, as a man whose great capacity for ambition had been misdirected.

The film was shot between February and April 2000 in Los Angeles. Johnny flew out with his family and they stayed at the house in Los Angeles. Throughout filming, Demme was often astonished by Johnny's acting. "Johnny Depp is a chameleon," he noted. "He, in my opinion, has never done the same performance twice. If you put 'Donnie Brasco' and 'Edward Scissorhands' and 'Ed Wood' in the same room and you told me that they were the same guy, I'd be hard-pressed to believe you. I knew that I wanted someone to transform into George. I didn't want a star playing a role in *Blow*. I wanted this guy to really wear the wigs and talk the talk, and do the whole thing. Johnny's one of the few guys, I think, in his generation that is willing to dirty himself up, if you know what I mean, to play a role. He brings all that, plus just the talent that all you guys know. He's a great actor, but his dedication is something that really, really impressed me a lot."

When Demme showed Jung a cut of the film, he couldn't believe it: "I showed George the rough cut. He was absolutely flipped out by Johnny. He had never seen a movie that Johnny had been in and Johnny nailed him to a 't' – the way he talks out of the side of his mouth, the way he walks with ass tucked in, the way he smokes, everything. Johnny went and spent a lot of time with him. So yeah, we were in a lawyer's holding room, very small and we had 14' TV with a VCR built into it. So it was me, the warden, George, a guard and my assistant in this tiny little room. In the last half-hour of the movie George went for a Kleenex and I knew we were in trouble. He just broke down and cried like a baby. Then I was crying, my assistant was crying, the warden was crying and the guard was crying, but trying to cover it up and act cool." (One headache with the role was the amount of cocaine Johnny had to mimic taking to play Jung accurately. To make the scenes authentic, he snorted a powdered baby laxative that made his nose stream and upset his stomach.)

Finishing work on *Blow* in April 2000, Johnny and family returned to France. Back on track with

Johnny nailed him to a 't. the way he talks out of the side of his mouth. the way he walks with ass tucked in. the way he smokes. everything.

major roles after the short hiatus surrounding his daughter's birth, he had already signed up for his next film, *From Hell* (2001), a depiction of London during Jack the Ripper's reign of terror. Set in 1888, he was to play "Inspector Fred Abberline", an opium-addicted detective on the trail of the Ripper. Fascinated by Jack the Ripper since stumbling across a documentary on TV at the age of eight, Johnny had since collected over twenty-five books about the case. Ever fascinated by the dark side of life, he jumped at the chance to do a "Ripper" film. As additional research, he took a Ripper tour of London with tour guide Donald Rumblelow, who said they ended up having a drink in the Ten Bells pub in Spitalfields, a place frequented by many of the Ripper's victims.

Co-directed by American fraternal team Albert and Allen Hughes and adapted from Alan Moore's graphic novel, the film was shot on a set built twenty minutes outside Prague in the Czech Republic between June

ABOVE: Johnny in Ted Demme's coke-dealing epic, *Blow*.

ABOVE: As opium-addicted Inspector Fred Abberline in *From Hell*.

ABOVE: Johnny with Vanessa Paradis and their daughter Lily-Rose.

and September 2000. Once again, Johnny brought his family over from France for the shoot. Starring opposite Heather Graham, he got along well with the Hughes Brothers, who had previously directed *Menace II Society* (1993) and *Dead Presidents* (1995). Allen Hughes described Johnny as "the sweetest person on the planet." The feeling was mutual. Johnny, at the time of the film's release, fondly recalled a moment when Allen gave great direction, "Allen gave me one of the most beautiful pieces of direction very subtly during a fairly large and tense scene. As an actor, each take you want to try something new to shake things up, so I was trying stuff. Allen came over after the take, leaned down and said into my ear, 'No sunshine.'"

With almost no overlap, Johnny went straight to work on his next project, which teamed him up again with Terry Gilliam. The director had conceived a film called *The Man Who Killed Don Quixote*, an epic based around events in the life of Don Quixote. When he first read the script, Johnny said he was "stupefied" by how

good it was. Both he and Vanessa Paradis committed to the film, which had a $34 million budget. Still in pre-production, Gilliam hired documentary makers Louis Pepe and Keith Fulton to chronicle the film's journey from seed to completion. They got plenty of material for the film was beset with problems. When, in September 2000, the cast assembled for the first day of filming on a set in northern Spain, a ferocious storm broke. The downpour reduced the desert terrains (necessary to the script) to a mudbath. Once the rain had dried out, by coincidence the location was also being used by NATO for target practice bombing raids! Then Jean Rochefort, one of the leading actors, who had to spend much of each day's filming on horseback, fell ill with a back problem and the whole project ground to a halt. Rochefort flew back to Paris to consult doctors and specialists. Investors and insurers nervously visited the set. Ten days later news reached the set that Rochefort had a double herniated disc and would have to pull out of the film. By then Gilliam had returned to London and the project collapsed. One of the last to leave, Johnny flew home soon after.

ABOVE: Depp as CIA agent "Sands" in the 2003 film, *Once Upon a Time in Mexico*.

Pepe and Fulton, the only members of the shoot with any luck, ended up editing their footage into the acclaimed documentary *Lost In La Mancha* (2002).

2001 was a quiet year by usual Johnny standards. He directed two promo videos for singles from Paradis' latest album *Bliss*: "Pourtant" and "Que Fait La Vie?". Then in May, he began work on his only acting job that year, playing CIA agent "Sands" in Robert Rodriguez' *Once Upon a Time in Mexico*. The film, which starred Antonio Banderas and Salma Hayek, was the third part of Rodriguez's "El Mariachi" trilogy and concerned

a plot to overthrow the Mexican government. Into this plot comes Sands with some pretty tall demands. Shot on location in Mexico, before filming Johnny decided he wanted to play Sands as a "bitter tourist." Rodriguez was fine with this. For him the main thrill of working with Johnny was seeing, "Johnny Depp doing action. Johnny's bad-ass – it's so cool to see." Again, as with action picture *Nick of Time*, Sands hardly ranked as one of his great performances. If anything, it was a bit of bubble gum, pure entertainment.

Once Johnny was finished in Mexico, he returned home to the South of France in July 2001. He enjoyed family life, telling one interviewer how he started days with his daughter: "I'd sweep her up in my arms

and we'd go to the orchard to pick a juicy peach for breakfast." This summer break soon extended into another sabbatical for Johnny after the couple learned Paradis was pregnant for a second time.

In February 2002 Johnny was shocked to hear that Ted Demme, the director of *Blow*, had died suddenly from a heart attack. Demme, who was thirty-seven, collapsed while playing a celebrity game of basketball, leaving behind a wife, a young daughter and a baby son. Johnny flew out to Los Angeles for the funeral that he described as "devastating." He himself just thirty-nine, he was shocked to lose a friend two years his junior.

On 9 April 2002 in Paris Paradis gave birth to a son at 1:30 a.m. They named him Jack John Christopher Depp III. Now with two children and living in a predominantly Catholic country, the couple were inevitably often asked if they were considering marriage. Johnny's standard retort was that they had no wedding plans because, "it would be a shame to ruin her last name. It's so perfect." In other interviews, he said the couple did sometimes discuss getting married but always came to the conclusion that they had been husband and wife in all but name ever since they moved in together. Conforming to tradition just for the sake of it was not of interest to them.

In June 2002, Johnny headed off once more, family in tow, for England, where he was to begin work on *Finding Neverland* (2004), a film directed by Marc Foster, that takes a fictional look at events that may have inspired Sir J.M. Barrie to write Peter Pan. Adapted from Allan Knee's play *The Man Who Was Peter Pan*, Johnny played "Barrie", whose life is re-shaped when he meets four boys and their young widowed mother, Sylvia Llewelyn Davies, played by Kate Winslet. As Winslet put it, "J.M. Barrie really came into Sylvia's life at a time when, you know, she'd dealt with a lot. Her own husband had passed away not long before and she was left with four children to deal with all on her own. And, you know, I think that he put happiness and affection back into her world."

LEFT: A scene from *Once Upon a Time in Mexico*.

RIGHT: Sir James Matthew Barrie wrote *Peter Pan* in 1904.

The idea behind Neverland is from your imagination make your dream life. I don't have to close my eyes to see it because I live with it every day.

ABOVE: Johnny drew on his recent experiences as a father for *Finding Neverland*.

BELOW: Acting opposite Kate Winslet in *Finding Neverland*.

ABOVE: Depp was charming in his role as the novelist Barrie.

The film gave Johnny an outlet for all his new experiences as a parent. Being around his two children all the time had changed his focus. Delighted, through Lily-Rose and Jack, to be living once more in the magical kingdom of childhood, he drew on this for the role of "Barrie". Director Marc Foster noticed during the shoot: "Johnny Depp has this beautiful sense about him of being, having this child within him alive. And he's so good with children. He just could fit right in there and play with them."

Johnny, who turned in a charming performance as Barrie of incredible feeling and sensitivity, ended up leaving the shoot far wiser from the work. Later he spoke in interviews of how the film had revealed to him the lucky place he had reached in his own life: "The idea behind *Neverland* is from your imagination make your dream life. I don't have to close my eyes to see it because I live with it every day: with my kids, my girl and my life. It's as perfect as it could possibly be."

CHAPTER TEN

CAPTAIN JACK

ABOVE RIGHT: Johnny as Captain Jack Sparrow in blockbuster *Pirates of the Caribbean: The Curse of the Black Pearl.*

When the filming of *Pirates of the Caribbean: The Curse of the Black Pearl* began in October 2002, Hollywood was surprised to learn that Johnny Depp, known for his gleefully offbeat choice of roles, was heading up the potential blockbuster. With a massive budget of $125 million and the intent to make the "best pirate movie ever", powerful producer Jerry Bruckheimer had especially sought him out for the role. "We needed an actor that said this is not just a Disney ride, that it's darker, edgier," the producer said. "So we went to France to convince Johnny to do it."

But Johnny was only too keen. Now the father to a son, he relished the opportunity to take on a role which he saw as being every boy's dream: to play at being a pirate. Disney cast him as Captain Jack Sparrow, whose mission in the film is to get his ship, *The Black Pearl*, back from the evil Captain Barbarossa, an old foe, who has stolen it. As ever, Johnny concocted a medley of obtuse references for the part, deciding to base his interpretation of Captain Jack on a combination of cartoon character Pepe LePew, a typical Rastafarian, and Rolling Stones guitarist Keith Richards. Before infusing Captain Jack with too much "Keith Richards", Johnny called the Rolling Stone, who he knew well, and asked for his endorsement. "He sent me a message to cover his behind," Richards said. "I've known Johnny for

'It was just a gas. It's probably the most centred and content I've ever been.'

ABOVE: Up close and personal with British actress Keira Knightley.

RIGHT: Johnny partly based Captain Jack on his friend, Rolling Stone Keith Richards.

a couple of years and he'd always pay for dinner. Now I realize that was his way of paying me for modelling."

For the role, Johnny had four of his teeth capped with gold and elected to sport a fake tattoo of a sparrow on his right arm. When filming ended, he had the sparrow tattooed permanently on his arm and added his son's name, "Jack", next to it. Earlier, he'd had his daughter's name, "Lily-Rose", tattooed over his heart. At this time, he had a total of eleven tattoos. Other than his mother's name and his children's names, he still had the infamous "Wino Forever" tattoo. Beyond these, he had the number three tattooed on his left hand between thumb and index finger, a symbol from *The Brave* on the inside of his right forearm and a skull and crossbones with the inscription "Death is certain" on his lower right leg. Also three mysterious rectangles

on his right index finger, an inverted triangle on his left bicep, another unknown symbol on his right ankle and his first ever tattoo (the head of a native American), which he got when he was seventeen, on his right bicep.

With Geoffrey Rush as Captain Barbossa, Orlando Bloom as Captain Jack's sidekick and Keira Knightley as the kidnapped governor's daughter, filming got underway. Initially, Johnny said his interpretation of Captain Jack had some people worried. Various high ranking Disney executives, lingering in the early days of the shoot, observed scenes, rushes and dailies and expressed their concern. They were unsure about the direction Johnny was taking with his portrayal of Captain Jack. His typical asides were along the lines of "What's he doing with his hand? Is the character a complete homosexual?" These anxieties raged

ABOVE: A sinister moment in *Secret Window*, adapted from a Stephen King novella.

RIGHT: Johnny suited the part of the reclusive artist, Mort Rainey, in *Secret Window*.

among the nervous executives for the first six weeks during which time they would regularly express their concerns to him. His standard reply was that he felt very sure of what he was doing and that they had to either trust him or replace him. When the film opened and became a massive box office success, Johnny said the same executives were calling to congratulate him. He said these calls were "deeply satisfying."

During the shoot, he found the stunts arduous. He said they were the hardest he had ever had to do. Previously, that accolade went to being dragged along the ground by a team of horses for *Sleepy Hollow*. In general though, Johnny's experience of working on a large budget aspiring blockbuster was a hugely positive one. "I really had a ball every single day," he said. "It was just a gas. It's probably the most centred and content I've ever been."

As yet unaware of just how huge *Pirates of the Caribbean: The Curse of the Black Pearl* was going to be, Johnny finished work on the film in March 2003 and took four months off. During this time, he signed up for *Secret Window* (2004), written and directed by David Koepp, based on a novella by Stephen King. Johnny was to star as Mort Rainey, a writer who suddenly finds himself accused of plagiarism by a demented fan played by John Turturro. After reading the script, Johnny felt compelled to do the film. The strength of the screenplay was down to Koepp, who had directed various low-key films, being best known for writing the screenplays for hit films like *Panic Room* (2002), *Mission Impossible* (1996), *Carlito's Way* (1993) and *Death Becomes Her* (1992). Aside from being seduced by the script, Johnny also wanted a change of gear after *Pirates of the Caribbean* and liked the fact that the role of Rainey was very much an internal one.

In June 2003, Johnny celebrated his fortieth

Johnny also wanted a change of gear after Pirates of the Caribbean and liked the fact that the role of Rainey was very much an internal one

birthday. His big concession to the milestone was to make a bid to cut down on smoking. The legendary smoker tried to reduce his heavy intake to a select few cigarettes per day. He said his new rules meant the first cigarette of the day came after lunch, the second after dinner and then he allowed himself a "luxury wild card" third and final cigarette, as and when the moment presented itself. Several months later, he would also start to work out regularly with a personal trainer. Both moves were sure signs that he was mellowing out, enjoying a new balance in life and that his family had made him feel grounded, brought him peace of mind. The self-destructive behaviour of the past seemed a lifetime away.

Filming of *Secret Window* began in July 2003. By then, Johnny had decided to model the character on Brian Wilson of The Beach Boys circa the making of *Smile* in 1966/1967, when Wilson, in the throes of emotional turmoil, covered his living room floor with sand and sat on this "indoors" beach writing beautiful songs on a baby grand piano. This sense of exile, of being reclusive was what Johnny wanted to import to the character of Mort Rainey: an artist living very much in his own imagination and universe. As ever, he impressed his director. Of working with Johnny, Koepp said: "He's a sponge, he picks up what's going on around him. Like that jaw thing that he does; I was doing that because I was grinding my teeth because I wasn't sleeping at night. So he just started doing it throughout the movie. You've got to be careful what you do around him because he'll steal it from you."

In July 2003, *Pirates of the Caribbean: The Curse of the Black Pearl* opened to unanimous acclaim and became a colossal box-office smash. The film went on to take $652 million worldwide, a vast return on its budget of $125 million. Harvey Weinstein, head of Miramax, whose Dimension Films co-financed *Once Upon a Time in Mexico* (2003), said of the film's success and its impact on Johnny's career, "I think he's been frozen out for years. I think he was looked at as too risky for a lot of the top stuff. A lot of people

LEFT: After *Pirates of the Caribbean*, Johnny took a cameo in *Ils se marièrent et eurent beaucoup d'enfants*.

are going to be kissing his butt now. But what they don't understand about Johnny is that he can smell BS ten miles away – the same guys, who a year ago were saying, 'Him? Are you kidding? He's box office poison.' Now he's the hottest thing in the universe."

Once Johnny finished work on *Secret Window*, he took a typically left-field turn. At a time when Pirates of the Caribbean was riding high and he could have chosen any role and commanded an astronomical fee, he instead spent a few days in November filming a cameo appearance in a French marital comedy called *Ils se marièrent et eurent beaucoup d'enfants* (2004). Written and directed by Yvan Attal, who also starred in the film opposite Charlotte Gainsbourg, Johnny appeared as a character titled "L'Inconnu". His role involved few words and a presence in only two scenes. Gainsbourg's character sees Johnny's character, a stranger, at a listening station in a record store and thereafter fantasizes about having an affair with him. Later in the film, he appears in a fantasy sequence. As usual, Johnny was keeping everyone guessing.

He entered 2004 at the top of his profession. *Once Upon a Time in Mexico* had opened in October 2003, riding the phenomenal success of *Pirates of the Caribbean: The Curse of the Black Pearl*. *Secret Window* was brought forward to capitalize on his stellar status and released in March 2004. The film was modestly successful, taking $47 million against a $40 million budget. *Ils se marièrent et eurent beaucoup d'enfants* fared less well. After premièring at the Cannes Film Festival in May 2004, the film would only achieve a limited release in the USA in 2005, grossing $252,000, a far cry from the takings of *Pirates of the Caribbean*.

At long last, for his performance as "Captain Jack" Johnny was nominated for an Academy Award in the Best Performance by an Actor in a Leading Role category. He went to the 2004 Academy Awards with Vanessa Paradis, but didn't enjoy the experience. "All Vanessa and I could think of was, when and where can we go smoke? And where can we get a drink? And when is it over? And please don't let me win. It was such a shock to get the news that I'd been nominated. My first reaction was, why? On one level I was flattered, but it's not what I'm working for. When

I didn't win the thing, oh, I was ecstatic, absolutely ecstatic. I applauded the lucky winner and said, 'Thank God.'" Although he lost out at the Oscars, he did win the Screen Actors' Guild award for Outstanding Performance by a Male Actor in a Leading Role.

Hitting such a peak of fame and wealth, Johnny reacted to the new level of intrusion on his personal life and privacy by buying an island. He was following in the footsteps of Marlon Brando, who had also once bought a deserted island to escape the cage of fame. While filming *Pirates of the Caribbean* in Tobago Cayes, Johnny had learned that a nearby 35-acre deserted island, Little Hall's Pond Cay, was for sale. After soliciting Brando's advice, he bought the island, which can only be reached by helicopter, boat or sea plane, for $3.6 million.

In spring 2004, just as *People* Magazine voted him the "Sexiest Man Alive", Johnny was back in England, family in tow, to start work on *The Libertine* (2004). The film, based on the life and times of John Wilmot, the Earl of Rochester, a debauched poet and bon vivant in the court of King Charles II, was shot on location in the Cotswolds. Johnny had been cast in the £8.7 million film as "Rochester", John Malkovich as King Charles II and Samantha Morton as Wilmot's mistress. The director, Laurence Dunmore, had struggled to make the film for years. "Johnny Depp has been involved with the project for about ten years," he said. "He went to see John Malkovich play 'Rochester' on the stage. We went back to Johnny because he was the only person I saw able to play Rochester the way I had in my vision. When he actually came to perform the role, it was obvious that he was born to play him." For Johnny, the role tapped into his past. He saw Rochester as a heavy drinker, a man medicating his inner demons. All Johnny had to do to get a handle on Rochester was flash back to the making of *What's Eating Gilbert Grape*. For additional research, he also spent time at The British Library in London reading up on the poet's life.

On 12 June 2004, Johnny announced that he had founded a new production company called Infinitum Nihil (Latin for "absolutely nothing") and that the company had signed a three-year, first-look production deal with the Initial Entertainment Group. What this meant was that Initial would finance and co-produce

films with Infinitum Nihil. Johnny was CEO of the new company and his sister Christie was president. The company was based in Los Angeles. By this time, Johnny had relinquished all business interests in The Viper Room and was focused on Infinitum Nihil and his shares in the Man Ray restaurants (John Malkovich and Sean Penn are also investors) in Paris and New York.

At around the same time, Johnny announced that he had signed up to lend his voice to Burton's animated film, *Corpse Bride* (2005). Burton described his film as "a love story that just happens to have skeletons." Johnny had taken the part of Victor Van Dort, who falls for Emily, the corpse bride of the title, whose voice would be that of Helena Bonham Carter. The character of Van Dort, a bumbling, sensitive oddball, was vintage Depp. By now, Burton wrote roles that were not only for Johnny, but steeped in his off-screen persona. Johnny saw similarities between "Van Dort" and "Edward Scissorhands", feeling neither was comfortable in the world, that both went through life feeling misunderstood, unable to communicate the important feelings they desperately wanted to get across.

On 1 July 2004 Marlon Brando died. Johnny was devastated. In various interviews, he paid tribute to his late friend and mentor, saying, "When we got together we were like children. We just laughed over completely just stupid and vile stuff: pee-pee, caca. fart stuff… And then sometimes there were great silences. He once told me he couldn't stand people that were afraid of silences. And he practised what he preached. We had great moments where we'd just sit and say nothing for an hour or two hours. Or there'd be a grunt, or look at that. But nothing more."

In June he went to work on yet another project with Tim Burton, a remake of the 1971 children's classic, *Willy Wonka and the Chocolate Factory*. Burton, who had earlier considered Michael Keaton and Christopher Walken for the part of Willy Wonka, eventually decided on Johnny in August 2003. As usual, his approach was casual. He invited Johnny to dinner and midway through the evening, mentioned that he

ABOVE: *Chocolate Factory* stars David Kelly, Johnny and Freddie Highmore with Tim Burton and producer Richard D. Zanuch.

RIGHT: Johnny as Willy Wonka.

was thinking of remaking *Willy Wonka* as *Charlie and the Chocolate Factory* and wondered if Johnny would be interested in playing "Willy Wonka". A long-time fan of Roald Dahl's work, Johnny didn't even have to think about it. As was always the case with Burton, he was instantly committed to the project.

Filming began on location in Hertfordshire, England. But Johnny was nervous about trying to live up to Gene Wilder's performance in the original. "I remember watching the film at home when I was a kid. It seemed to be on every year and I loved it," he said. "I've always loved Gene Wilder's work – *Young Frankenstein* and so on. Wilder's performance as Wonka was so definitive and seared into everyone's brains that I knew right away that I couldn't go anywhere near where he took the part."

Unusually for him, he arrived at the first day's filming without the character fully mapped

out. He had a good idea of where he wanted to go, but perhaps as a sign of his newly relaxed attitude to life, he allowed his portrayal of the character to unfold in the early days of filming.

"I wasn't nervous on my first day on set but it was tricky because Wilder had a very big pair of shoes to fill and that was a worry, but then you get to thinking, 'Well, why don't I just make another pair of shoes?' Just go outside of what Wilder did. Still salute and appreciate him but try to take it somewhere else. So I just worked with Tim, coming up with different ideas, and I gradually found a rhythm and strange logic to 'Willy'. I tried to find my own way into what I saw was the subversive side of the character, which is where I normally try to go with my work.

"During filming, every time a memory came up of that version of Wonka I would just veer left, radically. Also, we were working so closely

A long-time fan of Roald Dahl's work, Johnny didn't even have to think about it. As was always the case with Burton, he was instantly committed to the project

with what Roald Dahl had written in the book. We were really faithful to that and I kind of felt a deep sense of responsibility to Roald Dahl and his intent. That was important to me."

Johnny played the character as a "kind of game-show host cum bratty child," basing his interpretation on his memories of watching children's TV and how animated some of the hosts of those shows were. But many who saw the film were convinced that he borrowed heavily from Michael Jackson with his soft-voice, child-like wonder and strange mix of showmanship and acute embarrassment.

Johnny's children proved to be both a help and a hindrance when it came to peeling away Wonka's wrappers and getting under the skin of the man. "Children are always the most honest audience you'll ever get," he explained. "Whenever Lily-Rose and Jack would watch the Gene Wilder film on DVD, I

would immediately run out of the room because I didn't want to be influenced by his performance one way or the other. A lot of times what happens is you come up with these ideas and you never get to try them until a read-through. I often play Barbies with Lily-Rose. Sometimes I will put on an accent and she'll say, 'Daddy, don't use that voice.' Then we were playing one day and I started to use my Wonka voice, and she kind of lit up a little bit, like, 'Where's that coming from?' And I thought, 'All right, I think I'm on the right track here.'"

During the shoot, Burton made good use of time and had Johnny and Bonham Carter (who was also in *Charlie and the Chocolate Factory*) record their voice-overs for *Corpse Bride*. Such was the length of the shoot that it wasn't always possible for Vanessa Paradis and the children to be with Johnny. When they were in France, he missed them terribly. According to an insider on the set, "Every weekend is the same. On Friday night after work Depp takes a two-hour flight to Nice, followed by a two-hour drive to the family house in a tiny French village, then heads back to London again on Sunday night." This soon became routine as work on *Charlie and the Chocolate Factory* and *Corpse Bride* ran on to the end of 2004. He was also busy promoting *Finding Neverland*, which had opened in the autumn.

To the delight of millions of 'Captain Jack' fans around the world, Johnny entered 2005 by signing up to appear in not one but two sequels to *Pirates of the Caribbean: The Curse of the Black Pearl*. Commenting on why he would return to the role and put his name to a blockbuster trilogy, he said: "What happens to me is that once you've clicked into that character and you really know the guy you become very close and you love him. So it's always very difficult at the end. There is that week to 10 days before wrap where you can hear the clock ticking and then you go through a really nasty kind of depression afterwards. There's an odd separation anxiety because you've just been this person for a pretty good length of time and then they're suddenly gone. For me, with Captain Jack, I had a sneaking suspicion that I'd see him again and when they said, 'We'd like to do two and three together,' I was all for it because I wanted selfishly to be the guy again."

Soon after losing one mentor in Marlon Brando, Johnny lost another when Hunter S. Thompson committed suicide on 20 February 2005 by shooting himself in the head. A private memorial service was held at one of Thompson's regular haunts, the Hotel Jerome in Aspen, Colorado, on 5 March. It was decorated with an almost life-size black and white photo of the author and a large American flag. Johnny and fellow actor Bill Murray – who had portrayed Thompson in the movie *Where the Buffalo Roam* – made eulogies, along with Sean Penn, Jack Nicholson, John Cusack and Benicio Del Toro.

Johnny read a passage from Hunter's classic book *Fear and Loathing in Las Vegas*, and he had a police

ABOVE: Victor Van Dort gets hitched in Tim Burton's *Corpse Bride*.

ABOVE: Johnny with Hunter S. Thompson in 1998 at an event in New York where both read from *Fear and Loathing in Las Vegas*.

badge pinned to his jacket in tribute to the author's failed bid to become sheriff in 1970, when he ran his election campaign from the bar at the Hotel Jerome.

Later in the year, on 20 August, friends and admirers gathered at Thompson's ranch in Wood Creek, Colorado, for a private ceremony which captured the writer's wild and off-the-wall love for life. He had asked for his ashes to be fired from a cannon and had specifically requested that Johnny be the man to do it.

The cannon was fired from a 150ft tower topped by a red fist with two thumbs – the symbol of Thompson's free-wheeling, first-person gonzo journalism – whilst one of his favourite songs, Bob Dylan's "Mr Tambourine Man", was played. Red, white, blue and green fireworks were launched along with his ashes. It is understood that Johnny, in further tribute to Thompson, personally paid for the event, including the tower and cannon. "All I'm doing is trying to make sure his last wish comes true," Johnny

told the press. "I just want to send my pal out the way he wants to go out." Johnny would later say of Thompson, whose work had been such a big influence in his formative years, "He was a personal friend and a human being who changed my life in so many ways."

On 27 February 2005 Johnny was up for another Academy Award. He had earned a second nomination for Best Performance by an Actor in a Leading Role for his work in *Finding Neverland*. He was also nominated for a Golden Globe in the Best Performance by an Actor in a Motion Picture/Drama category for the film. But he failed to win either.

It would have meant little to Johnny anyway, who dislikes awards ceremonies. His approach has always been to learn his role, act it and then walk away from the movie both physically and mentally. "When I have finished work on a film I walk away. My job has been done," he has explained. It doesn't work quite like that of course, because there follows the round of interviews to promote the film. These he carries

ABOVE: Orlando Bloom, Keira Knightley and Johnny filming *Dead Man's Chest*.

out with admirable politeness and humility but you sense that this is the least appealing aspect of film making for him. A shy and private man, he is at odds with the movie star lifestyle and dislikes watching his own films. "I have a difficult time watching myself on screen," he has admitted. "In fact I have only ever watched a few movies that I have been in."

Never happier than at home with his family in France, Johnny spent quality time with them in the early part of the year as he prepared for the summer filming of the Pirates of the Caribbean sequels.

Now, happily making 'family movies', a contented Johnny spoke ever more of the healing nature of parenthood. "Kiddies give you strength and perspective," he told one reporter. "Things that would've made me upset or angry before, or things about Hollywood, in magazines or paparazzi, stuff like that, now you can go, 'Oh piss off – I'm going to play Barbies with my daughter!' And having a boy, I mean, it's really shocking, the differences between a little girl and boy. She's very elegant and everything has to be perfect and my boy, he stands up and screams like some god awful warrior, then runs straight into the wall."

That summer, as Johnny headed down to the Bahamas readying to shoot both sequels back to back, *Charlie and the Chocolate Factory* opened and became another massive Depp-Burton success, grossing over $200 million against an estimated

ABOVE: Rolling Stone Keith Richards agreed to play a cameo as Jack's father in *At World's End.*

budget of approximately $150 million.

Despite his worries, Johnny put in a memorable performance and made the character his own. He was enthusiastic in his admiration for Tim Burton and the book's author Roald Dahl, who both share a humour that is quirky, slightly sinister and occasionally gruesome! "I think there couldn't be a better combination of author and film maker than Roald Dahl and Tim Burton," he said. Johnny also went on to explain his on-going collaboration and friendship with Burton. "Tim's an old pal but at the same time he's a film maker that I admire so much. I am astounded by his

ability. What he's capable of is astonishing. We have a strange short-hand language between us that somehow works. We have a similar understanding of things that we consider absurd."

The pair fared well again that Autumn when *Corpse Bride* hit cinemas, grossing an acceptable $52 million against a $40 million budget. Meanwhile, Johnny was up to his neck in rum and yo-ho-ho bringing Captain Jack Sparrow back to life.

The story of *Pirates of the Caribbean: Dead Man's Chest*, saw Jack trying to wriggle out of a deal he once made to tortured soul Davy Jones – infamous captain of ghost ship, The Flying Dutchman – to hand himself over to his servitude. With Davy now demanding he make good on his promise, Jack has to find a way out of his debt or else be doomed to

ABOVE: *At World's End* opened worldwide on 25 May 2007, taking a record-breaking $401 million in its first six days.

eternal damnation and servitude in the afterlife.

The mammoth filming schedule meant that Johnny would need some breaks in between. On 16 September 2005 he flew to Los Angeles to follow many film legends before him and leave his hand prints in cement outside *Mann's Chinese Theatre* in Hollywood, another sign that he had been accepted by the Hollywood establishment. He also found time to pen an introduction to Gonzo, a limited edition monograph of photographs by Hunter S. Thompson.

The eagerly awaited *Pirates of the Caribbean: Dead Man's Chest* premiered on 24 June, 2006 and opened at cinemas worldwide on 3 July. It was another huge

box office success, grossing an estimated $423 million against a budget of $225 million. Again, Johnny's performance was lauded for its excellence. Over the opening weekend in the USA alone, the film grossed a staggering $135 million. The franchise could do no wrong. In the fanfare of the release, Disney proudly announced that Rolling Stone Keith Richards had finally agreed to play a cameo in the third film, as Captain Jack Sparrow's father.

Following a whirlwind of promotional duties, Johnny was back on board for the third instalment in August 2006, which would be called *Pirates of the Caribbean: At World's End*. This time a rather convoluted plot saw Lord Beckett (Tom Hollander), of the East India Dock Trading Company, now with control of Davy Jones's heart, forming an alliance with him to eradicate pirates. Jack, Captain Barbarossa, Elizabeth and Will, arrange a convention of the nine Pirate Lords with the intention of releasing the Goddess Calypso, Davy Jones's lover, from her human body of Tia Delma to face the powerful Davey Jones and Lord Cutler Beckett.

Johnny was delighted when his great hero and friend, Keith Richards, agreed to come on board. "God, it was great. He was just so cool," he recalled. "I mean, seeing Keith Richards arrive for work, totally prepared like, beautiful, at 7.30, 8 o'clock in the morning. It's like, 'What?' What a professional, man. He came in and just smoked us. He was amazing and adorable. This crew have been working together since 2002 when we began the first film and it's the first time that I'd seen the entire crew show up on set. So instead of 200 people it was like 500 or 1,000. We were all peeking, trying to get a glimpse of the maestro."

Johnny says that he and the crew were amazed by how easily and professionally Richards took everything in his stride. "He was like, 'Oh, so I stand here and say this and then I walk over here and do this,' and it was, 'Yeah, that would be great,'" he recalled. "And then it was two takes and Gore (director Gore Verbinski) was like 'Oh OK, next.' I started calling him Two-Take Richards."

Despite now being one of the biggest box office draws in the business, Johnny admits that he was still in awe of his childhood hero and the realisation that he was actually working alongside him would occasionally make him tongue-tied in his presence.

"We spent a bunch of time together but it would get to a certain point and I'd clam up," he said. "On one level there's this guy Keith and he's a terrific guy to hang out with and he's a really wonderful man. But there's always that sort of thing that reverberates within me – he is one of my guitar heroes and I can never escape that."

Johnny may have fantasised about jamming with his hero but he was far too in awe to suggest it. "We didn't jam together because I'm so miserably shy," he said. "The furthest I got was when he was showing me this mandolin-type instrument he uses in the film. I plunked a few chords on that and then

it was like, 'OK, thank you. I'm done.' And I gave it right back. I mean, he's a god. He's the master."

Pirates of the Caribbean: At World's End opened at cinemas worldwide on 25 May 2007. Once more it was a huge box office hit, attracting the highest ever tally in global box office takings for its first six days in cinemas. It grabbed a stunning $401 million, beating the $382 million six day total achieved by *Spiderman 3* earlier in the year. But whilst the *Pirates* continued to horde riches for Disney's overflowing treasure chest, many critics felt that the good ship had sailed one too many times. "Too much of a good thing," said one, whilst another described the script as "bloated and incoherent." But if the running time of 2hrs 48min might have tempted some to jump ship mid voyage, the fans still loved it and Johnny was saddened by the thought that it might be the last voyage. He admitted to shedding a few tears after finishing his last scenes. "I didn't want to say goodbye," he recalled. "It wasn't hysterical sobbing, but it goes deep into your body and into your soul. Captain Jack has brought a lot of good things into my world. I'll always hold him in very high regard."

Later, he delighted fans when he commented: "I've never really felt I'm done with playing the character, so why shouldn't we try a fourth and a fifth? If I were approached to play Captain Jack again, under the right circumstances, with all the right and proper elements involved and a good script, I would definitely give it some serious thought. There are things that crop up in your mind – 'flogging a dead horse' and 'gilding the lily' are two of them – but they don't apply from my perspective. It doesn't matter if the film makes a zillion dollars and breaks records, as long as it's for the right reasons."

In the meantime, Johnny had swapped his cutlass for a razor to play a far more sinister character....

RIGHT: Johnny joins a legion of film legends, leaving his marks in the pavement outside *Mann's Chinese Theatre* in Hollywood.

CHAPTER ELEVEN

JOHNNY SINGS!

ABOVE RIGHT: *Sweeney Todd* was the sixth movie on which Johnny had worked with director Tim Burton.

As soon as Johnny wrapped on *Pirates of the Caribbean: At World's End*, he headed straight to England in February 2007 to play the infamous London barber of legend, *Sweeney Todd*, in a movie version of Stephen Sondheim's stage musical. Once more, the director was his good friend, Tim Burton. In his colourful career, Johnny had shown his remarkable range with a succession of individual, frequently 'odd-ball' characters but with a shared sense of humanity and vulnerability. However, in *Sweeney Todd*, audiences were about to be shown yet another side to Johnny when he was to sing on screen for the first time.

The macabre tale of the London barber who cuts his customers' throats and has their bodies baked into pies by his Fleet Street neighbour, Mrs Lovett, was a perfect vehicle for a Depp-Burton collaboration – their sixth to date. Although there is no evidence of such a character having actually existed, the legend has fascinated people down the ages. Benjamin Barker, a 19th-century barber, arrives back in London after being sent to Australia following his wrongful conviction for a crime. He is then told his wife has killed herself and his daughter is the ward of his arch enemy, Judge Turpin (Alan Rickman). He changes his name to Sweeney Todd and starts to take revenge on all who have wronged him,

ABOVE: Despite having known him for years, Helena Bonham Carter had never heard Johnny sing.

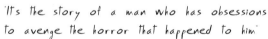

'It's the story of a man who has obsessions to avenge the horror that happened to him'

cutting his victims' throats with a razor before his friend and accomplice Mrs Lovett (Helena Bonham Carter), a pie shop owner, disposes of his victims in her pies. "It's the story of a man who has obsessions to avenge the horror that happened to him," Johnny explained. "I think we all secretly have that feeling in us but don't like to admit it. But I'm a big fan of revenge! It was challenging because there have been a lot of 'Sweeneys' over the years, so Tim and I sat down and thought about what this guy was going to look like and all of that. We knew this was a pretty special opportunity, a once-in-a-lifetime horror musical."

It certainly took him further out of his comfort zone than any other role and he had doubts about whether he could do it, but the challenge was irresistible, as Burton explained: "Every time Johnny and I work together, we try to do something different and I had never seen Johnny sing in the many years that I'd known him. We're always wanting to stretch ourselves, and this was a perfect outlet for that." But Johnny admits to being nervous at the prospect. "I've always been frightened of karaoke so I've never tried it. It scares the hell out of me," he said. "I've never even sung in the shower. I would be too mortified to do that."

ABOVE: Alan Rickman in the Demon Barber's chair on the *Sweeney Todd* set.

Although Johnny had actually been in the John Waters film musical *Cry-Baby* years earlier, in 1990, he was not required to sing. "Somebody else did the singing," he said. "I just acted. Sweeney Todd was the first time I had to do it and I really didn't know if I could pull it off. Tim was enormously brave to let me have a try." Even when he played guitar for The Kids, in Florida back in the 80s, he says he never actually sang an entire song. "I was the guy who would come in and sing the harmony, very quickly," he laughed. But it was to his old band mate, Bruce Witkin, who he turned to for advice. Witkin had been the singer and bass player in The Kids, and he was still involved in the music business, both playing and producing. He took Johnny along to a Los Angeles studio to record him singing "My Friends" from *Sweeney Todd*.

"I did it to see if I could get over my initial fear," Johnny later explained. "And I trusted Bruce to be honest with me on his verdict. That was the first song I ever sang in my life. It was pretty weird and scary. Afterwards, Bruce simply asked me, 'Do you want to hear the good news or the bad news?' I said, 'Well, give me the bad news.' And he said, 'The bad news is that you're going to have to do this.'" As filming got underway, high drama of another kind was about to strike. This time it was a real-life one which threatened the life of his beloved daughter, Lily-Rose.

ABOVE: Johnny greets Keith Richards at the première of *Sweeney Todd* **in New York.**

RIGHT: Johnny with Tim Burton who "hit pause" on the *Sweeney Todd* **set when Johnny's daughter was taken seriously ill.**

In March 2007, in the midst of filming *Sweeney Todd*, Lily-Rose fell critically ill, having caught an E.coli bacteria infection that caused kidney failure. She was rushed to London's renowned children's hospital, Great Ormond Street, and Johnny abandoned filming to keep a vigil at his daughter's side, along with Vanessa. After a tense nine days in hospital she was given the all

clear to leave but Johnny only returned to work when she had fully recovered, at the end of the month.

"I really wasn't sure if I'd be able to go back to the film," Johnny recalled. "Tim and the production crew were unbelievably supportive, and they said, 'Look, we're hitting pause.' For that, I'll be eternally grateful. It was without question the most frightening thing that we had ever been through. It was hell for us. But the magic is that she pulled through perfectly, beautifully. What got us through it wasn't the strength of Vanessa or me, but our daughter and her incredible ability to make us feel okay even though she was very unwell. She was super-strong. Amazing. And Great Ormond Street Hospital was terrific."

To show his appreciation, Johnny donated a million pounds to the hospital. He also invited five of its doctors and nurses to the première party of *Sweeney Todd* and, unknown to the public, spent four hours at the hospital telling bedtime stories to the sick children, dressed as Captain Jack.

"It was a very bumpy patch but she came through it unscathed and she is now as healthy as she always was," he later said. "It was a reminder to us of how lucky we are to be able to breathe, walk, talk, think and surround ourselves with people we love."

There was good news on the professional front when it was announced, on 13 December 2007, that *Sweeney Todd* had been nominated for four Golden Globes. Johnny was up for Best Performance by an

I really wasn't sure if I'd be able to go back to the film. Tim and the production crew were unbelievably supportive

Actor in a Motion Picture – Musical or Comedy, and his co-star Helena Bonham Carter was nominated in the female category. Tim Burton had a nomination for Best Director of a Motion Picture and the movie itself was up for Best Motion Picture – Comedy or Musical.

Sweeney Todd opened in the USA on 22 December 2007 and on 25 January 2008 in the UK before rolling out across the world. It was well received, although some critics thought that the film fell short of expectations (and by this stage expectations of Depp-Burton movies were considerably high). Reviews ranged from "disappointing" to "breathtaking." Another critic said: "Tim Burton was born to film this strange and spooky chamber piece."

Despite his worries, Johnny's singing was a revelation. His cockney tone was likened to that of David Bowie and Anthony Newley. But Johnny insisted that he wasn't trying to emulate anyone. "I wouldn't ever dream of attempting to channel David Bowie," he said. "He's a big hero of mine. If there's a similarity it wasn't intentional. It's a nice compliment anyway."

An on-going screenwriters' strike, involving a dispute over fees for shows broadcast on the internet, resulted in the Screen Actors Guild asking actors not to participate in the Golden Globes ceremony that year, in support of the writers. The ceremony was cancelled and demoted to a low-key, one-hour press conference on 13 January 2008 in which the winners were announced. Johnny and the film itself were both victorious.

Nine days later, further acclaim came his way when he was nominated for an Oscar for Best Performance by an Actor in a Leading Role. The screenwriters' dispute was settled in time for the glittering ceremony to take place on 24 February; in the event however, Johnny lost out to Daniel Day-Lewis for his performance in *There will be Blood*.

Johnny had narrated a film documentary called *Gonzo: The Life and Work of Dr. Hunter S. Thompson* towards the end of 2007 but the three-month screenwriters' strike from November meant that production of new movies and TV shows ground to a halt until it was resolved on 12 February

ABOVE: Fans gather for a glimpse of their hero at the London première of *Sweeney Todd* on 10 January 2008.

RIGHT: Living half the year in Los Angeles and half in rural France is ideal for Johnny, Vanessa and their children.

2008. This enforced 'time-off' was a welcome break for Johnny who played his favourite role of 'family man' once more back home in France.

Johnny is said to have bought Vanessa a vineyard in Provence in 2007 to celebrate her first album in seven years, *Divinidylle*, which she spent months recording in a French studio. It was released in January 2008 and she accompanied it with a sell-out tour of France and Belgium. When asked by a journalist how she spent a normal day, Vanessa replied, "There is no normal day. I take the kids to school. I might be touring. We spend half the time in France and half in the States where the kids go to school. In France they have a tutor. Our life is beautiful. We love each other. Everybody is healthy. We travel together. It's a fun ride."

Johnny shone further light on their 'nomadic' existence. "We live everywhere. We try to stay in France for six months a year, then we live in Los Angeles for six months. It has to do with my upbringing. I don't like to be stuck in one place for too long. We were total nomads when I grew up. We travelled around all the time. It's ingrained into my being. I think it's good for kids to get out there and see the world. There are other interesting places than just the United States."

But if France is one of Johnny's alluring mistresses, the UK is another. It's where many of his movies have been filmed, such as *Sleepy Hollow, Charlie and the Chocolate Factory* and *Sweeney Todd*. "I've always had a good thing with the Brits," he said. "It's the sense of humour. I've always felt 100 per cent at home in Britain and in London." He has become good friends with English comic actors Paul Whitehouse and Johnny Vegas, who he worked with in *The Libertine*.

British actor, Kevin McNally, who played first mate Joshamee Gibbs in *Pirates of the Caribbean: The Curse of the Black Pearl*, revealed that Johnny had picked up a lot of slang and colloquialisms from working so much with a British cast. "He's a great Anglophile and when he's on set he goes round saying 'mate' and 'bugger' and 'damn' all day long," he said. Johnny collects old documents and first-edition books and will

often set off, on his own, to historic places in Britain, whether it is to immerse himself in the environment and ambience for a role or simply for pleasure. "I'm fascinated by the history," he said. "I've loved taking weird little sojourns down to Bath or Rye or Chichester, or just wandering around Canterbury."

With the screenwriters' strike over, Johnny has been back working on various new projects. In March 2008 he began working on *Public Enemies*, set during the great crime wave of 1933–34, when the FBI cracked down on Depression-era criminals such as John Dillinger, Baby Face Nelson and Pretty Boy Floyd. Johnny plays the notorious bank robber Dillinger who was shot dead in an FBI ambush at the age of 31. The film was scripted by its producer, Michael Mann, and adapted from Bryan Burrough's book *Public Enemies: America's Greatest Crime Wave and the Birth of the FBI, 1933–34*.

Another project cropped up unexpectedly when the tragic death of Heath Ledger, in January 2008, left *The Imaginarium of Doctor Parnassus* unfinished. As a tribute to the *Brokeback Mountain* star, who died from an overdose of prescription drugs, Johnny joined forces with Colin Farrell and Jude Law to complete the film under the direction of Terry Gilliam. The three stars play different aspects of Heath's character, a travelling showman who sells his daughter to the devil for the gift of eternal life.

Following *Public Enemies*, Johnny is due to return to work on the postponed *Shantaram* which will be shot in India. He plays an Australian heroin addict named Lindsay, who breaks out of prison where he has been held for robbery, and reinvents himself as a doctor in the slums of Mumbai. Here he finds peace, running a free clinic but becomes involved in the crime underworld in his search for more medicine.

Then, the ever-more in demand actor stars in a film of Hunter S. Thompson's novel, *The Rum Diary*, about the life of freelance journalist Paul Kemp, who finds himself at a critical turning point in his life while writing for a run-down newspaper in Puerto Rico. Set in the late 1950s, the novel encompasses a tangled love story of jealousy, treachery and violent alcoholic lust among the American expatriates who staff the newspaper.

Thompson himself travelled from New York to San Juan, the capital of Puerto Rico, in 1960 to write for an ill-fated sports newspaper on the island. He had unsuccessfully applied to work at the larger English-language daily, the San Juan Star, but befriended many of the writers at the paper, providing the context for *The Rum Diary's* fictional storyline.

Johnny's production company, Infinitum Nihil, has bought the rights to the book, *Sasha's Story: The Life and Death of a Russian Spy*, about former KGB agent, Alexander Litvinenko, who died in mysterious circumstance in London in November 2006, when a large dose of radioactive polonium 210 was found in his body. Whilst critically ill in hospital, Litvinenko made a statement saying that he had been murdered by the Russian government following his criticism of the way the country was being run.

Ironically, for someone who has been known for choosing smaller artistic films over commercial blockbusters, Johnny is now at the top of the league of box office draws. In 2007 he was voted the top moneymaking star by US cinema owners for the second year running. Captain Jack Sparrow has turned him into a mainstream super-star, and netted him a tidy fortune along the way. But he has done this without compromising a grain of integrity, choosing the character over 'pay packet' every time.

"I was the guy who had been bouncing around the film industry for years and years and I'd been lucky if five or 10 people would see my movies," he said. "So Captain Jack did a big flip for my career. He and the *Pirates of the Caribbean* experience have afforded me and my family a certain luxury in that we are able to live a little more comfortably and it will reverberate for my kids and their kids. When I decided to take the role, it was pure instinct. I didn't know it was going to be such a huge hit."

But Johnny played Captain Jack 'his way' to the initial nervousness of Disney executives and continues to be a maverick in his approach to his work. His success and wealth means that he has the luxury to be ever more choosy in his roles.

At the age of 44 he says he is "far more mellow" than ever before. "I can handle things. It's me who

is in control now. I almost feel guilty about being so happy. You start to think that there's something terrible waiting for you around the corner, and then you take a peek and all you see are palm trees and your family. I'm still cynical about things, but I don't have a dark vision of the world any more. I have learnt to grow up and still enjoy myself. I spent a lot of years living on the edge – everyone knows that. So it's good that I live calmly and happily.

"At the age of 12, I felt it was me against the world. I remember locking myself in my bedroom and playing my guitar. It seemed as if I was in there for about two or three years. The most important thing is that now, at least, I feel comfortable with myself. I don't have to pretend any more about who I am. I don't want to portray any image that isn't myself."

Becoming a father made him even more determined to do work that not only he but also his children could be proud of. "I was always making choices about what movies to do but after my kids were born I decided that I was not going to do anything that could be potentially embarrassing for them later, when they watch," he said. "I don't want them to be ashamed."

At the peak of his career and with the family life he has always longed for, Johnny knows where his priorities are, as he has pointed out: "I think we are very lucky. My kids are very well balanced, very grounded. My family is my sanctuary. I live for them now. I finally found a reason to exist in this world. There is nothing like it. I would give everything away, if I could only keep my family."

And what of the future? "I'm an old-fashioned guy," he recently said. "I want to be an old man with a beer belly sitting on a porch, looking at a lake or something."

SOURCES

Material from the following titles and periodicals informed the researching of this book: *TV Guide, Splice, Model, Rolling Stone, Premiere, Entertainment Weekly, Uncut, Vanity Fair*, the *Observer*, the *Evening Standard*, the *Independent, GQ, Sky, Esquire, Playboy, Total Film, Time Out, Vogue, Elle, The Face, Seventeen*, the *Guardian, Interview, Sassy, Movieline, Details, Time, USA Today*, the *Daily Telegraph, Hot Dog, Neon* and the *Sunday Mail*.

The publishers would like to thank the following sources for their kind permission to reproduce the pictures in this book.

© **BBC:** 140

Corbis Images: /Thierry Orban: 81; /Picturescope International: 77; /Frank Tapper: 9

Getty Images: /James Aylott: 74-75; /Frank Driggs Collection: 15; /Deborah Feingold: 32; /Hulton Archive: 109; /David Keeler: 65; /Robin Platzer/ Twin Images/Time Life Pictures: 36; /Time Life Pictures: 18, 51b, 76

Photos 12: /Collection Cinema: 31, 38, 62-63, 90, 99

Redferns: /GAB Archives: 23

Retna Pictures Ltd.: /Erik Auerbach: 13; /Steve Granitz: 44; /Robert Matheu: 8, 17

Rex Features: 12, 16t, 61, 64, 80, 94, 95, 110b, 111, 124-125, 138; /Alex Berliner/BEI: 131; /Cesare Bonazza: 59; /Peter Brooker: 52; /Stefania D'Alessandro/BEI: 137; /Everett Collection: 4-5, 14, 19, 20, 24-25, 26, 28, 33, 34, 35, 40b, 42b, 45, 49, 54, 55, 56, 57b, 68-69, 71, 72, 78, 79, 82-83, 85, 86 87b, 92, 93, 96-97, 100, 101, 102, 104-105, 132, 133, 135; /Everett Collection/20th Century Fox: 41t, 41b, 42t, 105br; /Everett Collection/ Artisan: 91; /Everett Collection/Buena Vista: 128, 129; /Everett Collection/Columbia: 107, 108, 116, 117; Everett Collection/Dreamworks: 134; /Everett Collection/Miramax: 66tl; /Everett Collection/Tristar: 21; / Everett Collection/Universal: 39, 40t, 98; /Everett Collection/Walt Disney: 112, 113, 114, 115, 127; /Everett Collection/Warner Bros: 123, 126 left; /Albert Ferreira: 136; /Jag Gundu: 121; /Keystone USA: 110t; /Erik Pendzich: 126 right; /Kore Press: 106; /PORVA: 60; /Brian Rasic: 11; /Tim Rooke: 53; /Karl Schoendorfer: 16b; /Sipa Press: 70, 73, 87t, 89, 118, 139; /Jim Smeal: 2, 88; /Snap: 27, 30, 46-47, 48, 50, 51t, 57t, 58, 66-67; / Unimedia International: 22; /Richard Young: 7, 122; /Vinnie Zuffante: 127, 143

Every effort has been made to acknowledge correctly and contact the source and/or copyright holder of each picture and Carlton Books Limited apologises for any unintentional errors or omissions, which will be corrected in future editions of this book.